NHS

Modernising Medical Careers

Operational framework for foundation training

London: TSO

Published by TSO (The Stationery Office) and available from:

Online
www.tso.co.uk/bookshop

Mail, Telephone, Fax & E-mail
TSO
PO Box 29, Norwich, NR3 1GN
Telephone orders/General enquiries: 0870 600 5522
Fax orders: 0870 600 5533
E-mail: book.orders@tso.co.uk
Textphone 0870 240 3701

TSO Shops
123 Kingsway, London, WC2B 6PQ
020 7242 6393 Fax 020 7242 6394
68-69 Bull Street, Birmingham B4 6AD
0121 236 9696 Fax 0121 236 9699
9-21 Princess Street, Manchester M60 8AS
0161 834 7201 Fax 0161 833 0634
16 Arthur Street, Belfast BT1 4GD
028 9023 8451 Fax 028 9023 5401
18-19 High Street, Cardiff CF10 1PT
029 2039 5548 Fax 029 2038 4347
71 Lothian Road, Edinburgh EH3 9AZ
0870 606 5566 Fax 0870 606 5588

TSO Accredited Agents
(see Yellow Pages)

and through good booksellers

Published for the Department of Health under licence from the
Controller of Her Majesty's Stationery Office.

First published 2005

ISBN 0 11 703546 7

Table of contents

Table of contents

Table of contents

Modernising Medical Careers (MMC) is a UK wide strategy to reform postgraduate medical education. MMC, published by the four UK Health Ministers in 2003, will deliver a postgraduate education strategy that is based around clearly defined clinical and non-clinical competences and works towards a process of lifelong professional development.

The first component of this modernised training programme for doctors will be the two-year Foundation Programme, a planned programme of supervised clinical practice designed to provide a bridge between undergraduate and postgraduate medical training.

The *Operational Framework for Foundation Training* has been developed to help support the implementation and delivery of foundation training that will commence across the UK in August 2005. From that date it is anticipated that all UK medical graduates will undertake a two-year Foundation Training Programme. The *Curriculum for the Foundation Years in Postgraduate Education and Training* sets out the content and competences that need to be achieved and demonstrated through assessment during this period of training. The *Operational Framework* is a companion document to the *Curriculum* and should be used in conjunction with it.

The NHS cannot afford to loose this opportunity to ensure that doctors are specifically trained, early in their careers, to provide safe patient care and are confident in managing acutely ill patients. Implementation of this early phase of Modernising Medical Careers will allow new graduates to work and learn in carefully planned programmes which will give them access to structured and managed training. This *Framework* is designed to help Postgraduate Deans in partnership with Medical School colleagues, Clinical Tutors, Foundation Training Programme Directors (FTPDs), the NHS, and others implement foundation training across the UK.

This *Framework* will need adaptation for the contexts, organisation and terminology appropriate for each of the devolved administrations. In addition, this *Framework* will be subject to early review in 2007, in response to and along with a parallel review of the foundation *Curriculum*.

The enormous contribution of the Postgraduate Deans to the development of this *Framework* is gratefully acknowledged.

Section A
Introduction

1   *Modernising Medical Careers (MMC)* is a broad policy statement from the four UK Health Ministers that was published in February 2003. It sets a new direction for postgraduate medical education, reflecting the formal consultation on the proposals originally set out in *Unfinished Business: reforming the SHO grade.*

2   These proposals aim to ensure high levels of patient safety, and the delivery of better standards of patient care by improving the effectiveness of healthcare teams and developing medical practitioners who are accountable and sensitive to the needs of patients and the NHS as they progress in their careers.

3   The concept of **Foundation Training Programmes** (FTPs), encompassing the current pre-registration year and the first year of post-registration training, is one of the most fundamental and innovative proposals of MMC. This *Operational Framework* sets out the parameters within which Foundation Training Programmes will develop under the auspices of the four UK Health Departments, the General Medical Council (GMC), the Specialist Training Authority (STA) and the Joint Committee on Postgraduate Training for General Practice (JCPTGP - until September 2005), the Postgraduate Medical and Education Training Board (PMETB – from September 2005) and the Postgraduate Deans. The GMC and PMETB are responsible for setting the standards of training, whilst the Postgraduate Deans are responsible for managing the delivery of training to meet the standards set by the GMC and PMETB.

4   The *Curriculum for the Foundation Years in Postgraduate Education and Training* was published in April 2005. It sets out the outcomes and competences required by the end of foundation training. This *Operational Framework* has been developed in response to it, to help support its implementation by the Postgraduate Deaneries, Clinical Tutors and local health communities through which foundation training is commissioned.

5   The *Framework* has been developed in the full recognition of the differing organisational structures in the four home countries. It therefore identifies key issues and, in some areas, provides recommendations for a set of overarching operational principles for foundation training. However, it is structured to enable each country to develop nationally modified *Operational Frameworks* to take into account different organisational structures, practice and terminology. It is anticipated therefore that each country will adapt this Framework for its local circumstances, whilst adhering to the overarching principles within it.

6   Implementation of Foundation Training Programmes will take place from August 2005. From that time, it is anticipated that all UK medical graduates who have not yet undertaken pre-registration training will apply for entry to a two-year Foundation Programme following graduation. The first foundation year (F1) will replace the current pre-registration house officer (PRHO). Successful completion of F1 will result in full registration with the GMC. This will be followed by a second foundation year (F2), characterised by specific and defined educational objectives. Non-UK graduates who require a provisional year in order to obtain registration with the GMC will be eligible to apply competitively for admission to a two-year Foundation Programme.

7   *Modernising Medical Careers, the Next Steps: The future shape of Foundation, Specialist and General Practice Training Programmes* further sets out the strategic direction of postgraduate medical education. Its Annexe two, *A Firm Foundation (www.mmc.nhs.uk)*, describes the standards for foundation training, and emphasises that the Foundation Programme will be *'the bridge between undergraduate medical training and specialist and general practice training'*.

8   The new policy direction heralded by *Modernising Medical Careers* needs to be placed firmly within the context of the General Medical Council's *Good Medical Practice* (GMP).

9   *Good Medical Practice* sets out the standards of clinical and professional performance expected of the medical practitioner. Appendix 1 sets out the *Duties of a Doctor* registered with the GMC. All doctors should be aware of GMP, not only because these are the standards against which a medical practitioner's performance will be judged throughout their professional life, but also because adherence to them will ensure that patients receive high standards of safe and effective healthcare.

Section B
Guiding principles of Modernising Medical Careers

10   There are four key underlying educational principles to *Modernising Medical Careers* that set the context for Foundation Programmes.

Outcome based: *Modernising Medical Careers* makes clear that outcome based learning and training will mark a key change in the direction of postgraduate medical education. Trainees must achieve **explicit incremental standards** at each stage of training in order to progress.

Defined Competence: These outcomes define in broad terms what the doctor can be expected to offer as a professional upon completion of the training programme. However, they can be refined and clarified by identifying the outcomes in terms of specific competences that are defined by clear waypoints which mark when they have been achieved. At each stage of training there should be clarity about the areas of competence to be reached.

Assessment of Competence: One of the new messages of *Modernising Medical Careers* is about the assessment of competence and performance in various defined clinical and professional areas of practice. Since assessment drives learning, the introduction of assessment that looks at the core competences (competency-based assessment) at all stages of postgraduate medical education signals a major educational development.

Professional development and life-long learning: *Modernising Medical Careers* is clear about the need for doctors to develop an approach that enables flexibility within their careers so that they can respond to an ever-changing health environment. This need for life-long learning, career development and reflection should be placed within the context of professional development as described in *Good Medical Practice.* *Modernising Medical Careers* highlights, for example, excellent team working skills as key to professional behaviours that will support patient safety and good clinical care. As part of this approach, *Modernising Medical Careers* also makes an explicit commitment to supporting the development of those who want to pursue an academic career.

11   Underpinning these principles is the recognition that a robust educational *Framework* will be required to support the delivery of the training programmes and the individuals undertaking them. This *Framework* should, however, be set within the context of learning from patients and professionals within the workplace. Training, education and learning must coexist with the care and service provided to patients. The healthcare system has two core functions:

   i   to promote good health and provide healthcare (in the widest sense and including research and development) to those who require it today; and

   ii   to promote good health and provide healthcare for the generations to come

This second responsibility cannot be met unless the service and training tensions of the past are resolved. It is the responsibility of government, the NHS and educational leaders to address these tensions to enable a **learning environment** that supports both the delivery of healthcare and the training of the next generation of healthcare professionals. This includes developing an educational faculty that is appropriately trained to deliver foundation training.

All foundation training will be set within a structured Foundation Training Programme (FTP), reflecting the move of postgraduate medical education in the UK from experiential training in a series of posts to a structured programme of training which is also experientially based, but managed within a coherent *Framework* of training. This reflects the changes that have already taken place in specialist training.

12   The underlying educational principles of Foundation Training Programmes can now be identified within the context set by these *Modernising Medical Careers* principles.

Outcomes: From August 2005 it is anticipated that all UK medical graduates who wish to obtain full registration will undertake a two-year Foundation Programme, the first year of which will be a pre-registration year (F1) and a second year which will be a post-registration year (F2). Clear outcomes and competences for each foundation year have been identified by the General Medical Council (GMC) and PMETB for F1 and F2. These have formed the basis of the combined *Curriculum for the Foundation Years in Postgraduate Training and Education*, supported by the GMC and Postgraduate Medical Education and Training Board (PMETB). The *Curriculum* will be reviewed during the early implementation of foundation training.

The GMC has published its new edition of *The New Doctor (2005)* (available at *http://www.gmc-uk.org/med_ed/default.htm*). This will be developmental, with full implementation of the defined outcomes and competences expected by 2007. It describes the outcomes that must be demonstrated by a provisionally-registered doctor after August 2007 before they are granted full registration at the end of the F1 year. Until 2007, the GMC will continue to grant full registration when a PRHO completes 12 months in posts approved for PRHO training. At least three months training must be completed in medicine and another three months in surgery, and a Certificate of Experience completed. Programme providers are empowered to deliver the outcomes set out in *The New Doctor* from 2005 and they must deliver these outcomes by 2007.

The overall outcomes of the F2 year (first year post-registration) are defined in *Modernising Medical Careers*. These 'aim to imbue trainees with basic practical skills and competences in medicine and will include:

- effective relationships with patients
- high standards in clinical governance and safety
- the use of evidence and data
- communication
- team-working
- multi-professional practice
- time management
- decision making
- an effective understanding of the different settings in which medicine is practised'

Defined Competence: The specific aims and objectives of foundation training are to enable the new medical graduate to:

- develop further and consolidate clinical skills, particularly with respect to acute medicine so that sick patients are regularly and reliably identified and managed, in whatever setting they present

- ensure that professional attitudes and behaviours are embedded in clinical practice

- validate the acquisition of competence in these areas through a reliable and robust system of assessment

- offer the opportunity for doctors to explore a range of career opportunities in different settings and areas of medicine

Section C
Principles of Foundation Programmes – outcomes and competences

Foundation training is a formal introduction into the world of work for the medical graduate and is designed to bridge the gap from being a medical student to becoming a doctor fit to work within the NHS. The *Curriculum (www.mmc.nhs.uk)* identifies the core competences, which doctors should normally obtain within two years of graduating from Medical School. These will be assessed using tools developed in accordance with the principles and standards of assessment laid down by the competent authorities for foundation training, the GMC and the Postgraduate Medical Education and Training Board (PMETB). Foundation doctors will be required to demonstrate the achievement of the foundation competences and to complete two years of experiential foundation learning.

Professional development and life-long learning: All doctors undertaking foundation training will need to develop their understanding and skills in self-directed and reflective learning in order to support their professional development. The need to maintain and develop professional behaviours throughout a lifetime of work starts with foundation training and will be re-affirmed through revalidation of their professional standing and registration on a regular basis. This is designed both to support the foundation doctor in making appropriate career choices, but also to support the development of attitudes which are sufficiently flexible to enable adjustments to working practices, and indeed, to career focus, where this may be required. This is but one of the professional attributes that trainees will need to demonstrate. Based on the professional requirements of *Good Medical Practice (available at http://www.gmc-uk.org/standards/good.htm)* and *Continuing Professional Development* (available at *http://www.gmc-uk.org/med_ed/cpd/guidance.htm*), a generic learning programme to support professional development focused on patient safety and accountability through clinical governance is described in paragraphs 148 – 157.

13   The learning environment for Foundation Programmes will be characterised by it being:

- trainee-centred
- competency assessed
- service-based
- quality-assured
- flexible approach
- coached
- structured and streamlined training

The NHS has, however, a clear patient-focused ethos. The trainee-focus of *Modernising Medical Careers* must be reconciled and integrated with this. This *Framework* will describe in some detail what is needed to create the educational environment to deliver the outcomes of Foundation Training Programmes.

14 The General Medical Council is the competent authority for determining the patterns of experience which may be recognised as suitable for the completion of basic medical education, leading to full registration. This is pre-registration training and it is envisaged that it will be undertaken during the first year of the Foundation Programme. The GMC also has a statutory duty to promote high standards and co-ordinate all stages of medical education as well as specific roles in relation to undergraduate medical education and quality assurance. Its authority and responsibilities are set out in the Medical Act 1983. All doctors must be registered with the GMC before working as a doctor in the UK. (Further information about registration is available on the GMC website at *http://www.gmc-uk.org*)

15 The GMC, which has responsibility for F1, and the PMETB, which has responsibility for F2, are working together to ensure the creation and maintenance of co-ordinated structures for this period of training including setting standards and quality assurance.

16 The Postgraduate Medical Education and Training Board (PMETB) is the competent authority responsible for setting the standards and for quality assuring postgraduate medical education across the UK following full registration and completion of basic medical education. Its authority and responsibilities are laid down in *The General and Specialist Medical Practice (Education, Training and Qualifications) Order 2003*.

17 In conjunction with the GMC, the PMETB is responsible for setting the standards of training to be delivered by Foundation Training Programmes and for quality assuring these. *Modernising Medical Careers: the Next Steps* acknowledges that 'the term **"programme"** will mean different things to different stakeholders' (paragraph 13). PMETB has defined 'programme' as a 'defined period of managed, supervised training.'

18 Paragraph 15 of Next Steps states that 'the best definition of a "programme" is in terms of a unit of approval composed of a series of rotations and placements which is educationally viable and convenient to manage. Such units of approval will have the capacity to encompass a number of trainees.' The PMETB Rules (*www.pmetb.org.uk*) support this concept that is fundamental to developing the structure and approach that will support foundation training. The 'unit of approval' by the PMETB will therefore be a Foundation Training Programme with approximately 20 – 40 F1 and F2 one-year training opportunities (posts) that will be managed by the Foundation Training Programme Director, or Foundation Training Programme Tutor (FTPD/T), accountable to the Postgraduate Dean for the quality and delivery of training.

19 The GMC and PMETB have identified that, as a matter of principle, they will want to move to approving programmes and that the level at which they propose to engage with education providers for purposes of approval will be that of the **Postgraduate Deanery**.

20 Hence **all** foundation training will be delivered within a **Foundation Training Programme (FTP)** led by a **Foundation Training Programme Director/Tutor (FTPD/T)**. As detailed below there will be three types of appointments into Foundation Training Programmes:

- two year appointment to encompass F1 and F2 training
- one year appointment to F1 (first year of foundation training)
- one year appointment to F2 (second year of foundation training)

21   The Postgraduate Deaneries have operational responsibility and accountability for ensuring that the Foundation Programme is delivered to the national standards set by the GMC and the PMETB.

22   Deaneries will need to ensure that there is an effective educational infrastructure to support the Foundation Training Programme development by establishing **Foundation Schools**, which are responsible for the operational aspects of delivering Foundation Training Programmes. The details of implementation will vary between and within the four countries. An outline structure is described below.

Foundation Schools – overall structure

23   Foundation Schools will operate under the auspices of the Postgraduate Deans who will develop, in conjunction with the university and Medical School/s in the Deanery, the educational supportive *Framework* described below. In addition, close working with provider organisations will be essential to develop and maintain such supportive environments.

24   Overall accountability for the quality of training delivered through the School will rest with the university and the Postgraduate Dean with particular responsibility for the F1 year falling to the university.

25   Quality assurance (QA) for foundation training will be through a joint approach to be established by the GMC and the PMETB, which will quality assure the Foundation Training Programmes overseen by the Deaneries. Deaneries will quality control the delivery of foundation training through monitoring of educational contracts with NHS employers.

26   **Deaneries/Foundation Schools** will support a structure to enable the GMC and PMETB to undertake an effective review of the quality of the training delivered. To achieve this, Deaneries/Foundation Schools will identify a number of Foundation Training Programmes within the Deanery/School. Each **Foundation Training Programme** will usually support no more than 20 - 40 combined F1 and F2 training opportunities (posts) providing foundation training, but this may vary between the four countries. Foundation Training Programme Directors/Tutors (FTPD/T) should be appointed to lead Foundation Training Programmes. Normally one FTPD should manage 20 – 40 F1 and F2 posts and the trainees in them. The Clinical Tutor/Director of Medical Education may be appointed a FTPD since many of their current responsibilities with respect to PRHOs/F1s and first year SHOs/F2s will be subsumed in the role of FTPD.

27   Deaneries may wish to establish a **Foundation School Management Committee** or a **Deanery Foundation School Board** (especially where there is more than one School in a Deanery), to oversee and set the strategic direction of the School/s, although this will vary between the four countries. Where a Board is established, it is likely to comprise:

- the Postgraduate Dean/s (Chair)
- the Director/s of Postgraduate General Practice Education
- the Dean of each Medical School linked to a Foundation School

- the Directors of each of the Foundation Schools
- an NHS chief executive from each School
- a lay representative
- a trainee representative from each Foundation School
- others as deemed appropriate by local circumstances

28 The **managerial** unit within each School responsible for local delivery of foundation training is the **Foundation Training Programme** consisting of between 20 – 40 F1/F2 training opportunities (one-year posts), although the size will ultimately need to conform to the requirements of the PMETB with respect to approval of Foundation Training Programmes. The details of the structure and resourcing within a School will vary from country to country, e.g. a Deanery with a single Foundation School will not require a separate Deanery Foundation School Board but may set up a Foundation School Management Committee or equivalent.

Foundation Training Programmes – led by (FTPD/T)

- usually no more than 20 - 40 training opportunities
- the Foundation Training Programme is the unit of review for quality assurance by GMC/PMETB

Foundation School – led by School Director

- under the auspices of identified Postgraduate Deanery
- will have several hundred F1 and F2 doctors participating in **individual foundation programmes (ifp)**
- may be several per Deanery
- overseen by a **Foundation School Management Committee** chaired by the School Director; membership to include the FTPDs within the School (or a representative number), Deanery, Medical School, local health services, trainee and lay representation

Deanery Foundation School Board – chaired by Postgraduate Dean

- oversees and sets overall strategy for the Foundation Schools in a Deanery in line with national standards
- ensures consistency across Schools in Deanery
- has representation from the Deanery, Medical School, health services, Foundation Schools, lay and trainee membership

29 Trainees undertaking a two-year foundation training as well as those who undertake one-year F1 or F2 appointments will each follow an **individual foundation programme (ifp)**. Training for both two-year appointments and one-year appointments all take place within **Foundation Training Programmes**, under the auspices of the Foundation Training Programme Director/Tutor. individual foundation programmes will be made up of three, four or six-month **placements**, offering a range of training experiences and opportunities.

30 At each level, there will need to be sufficient administrative and infrastructure support to allow training and education to progress smoothly for the trainee. Appendix 2 sets out a model generic job description for the Foundation Training Programme Director/Tutor (FTPD/T) that could form the basis for appointment to these roles, with national and local variation where appropriate. FTPD/Ts should normally be joint appointments, made by the local NHS (usually the Trusts/hospitals) and the Deanery.

31   Responsibility for the delivery of foundation training and for foundation trainees is shared between the Deanery and the Health Service employer.

32   The Deanery has overall **educational responsibility** for the trainees and for locally quality assuring the standards of education delivered. It will need to develop effective partnerships with Medical Schools, other Deaneries and local health services to optimise delivery of foundation training.

33   NHS Trusts have **employer responsibilities** with respect to doctors in foundation training.

34   In England, but not elsewhere, **Foundation Trusts** which will be involved in training foundation doctors must ensure that they deliver training to the standards set by the PMETB and as agreed locally in the Postgraduate Deans' educational contract (see below).

Educational responsibilities

35   These requirements are laid out in the Educational Contract which is embodied in the commissioning arrangements between the Deanery/Foundation School and the Trust. The educational contract sets the agreed standards for foundation training in a local context. A generic model is attached in Appendix 4. The Deanery has the specific role for local quality control of foundation training in order that the competent authorities can fulfil their overall quality assurance roles. The Deanery achieves quality control through the monitoring of training provided under the terms of its Educational Contract and the standards laid down within it.

36   Table one lays out a *Framework* structure that identifies the potential roles of educational leads and briefly defines their roles and responsibilities. The details of this will need to reflect the organisational structure for foundation training that is developed within each of the four countries.

Employer responsibilities

37   NHS Trusts/Hospitals are the employers of foundation trainees. As such, they have employer's responsibilities for:

- meeting the terms and conditions of doctors in foundation training, including hours of work and payment for banding arrangements
- ensuring a safe working environment
- protecting staff from bullying and harassment
- ensuring an environment which respects diversity and equality of opportunity
- undertaking employer responsibilities for disciplinary action with respect to conduct and performance
- ensuring that postgraduate education is delivered in an environment which supports learning and meets educational standards
- supporting the training of trainers so that they are competent to deliver effective postgraduate education

38   Deaneries and NHS employers must work effectively together to ensure that doctors in foundation training learn and work to the benefit of both patient care and safety, and their own professional development.

Section F
Roles and responsibilities

Table 1 - The Educational Infrastructure Supporting Foundation Training
(*Framework* model to be modified as appropriate for each national/Deanery structure)

	Purpose	Responsibilities	Structure
Foundation Training Programme (FTP)	To ensure local delivery of training and education for foundation trainees	Responsible for the delivery of foundation training for foundation trainees	Appropriately trained **Foundation Programme Training Directors or Tutors (FTPD/Ts)** should be appointed to lead each **Foundation Training Programme**
	Will be responsible for the day-to-day delivery of foundation training	Coordinates activities to ensure delivery of Foundation Programme training, including the formal generic component of the training programme	Administrative support reflecting the overall number of Foundation Training Programmes should be appointed to support the FTPD/T
	The **Foundation Training Programme** is the unit of approval to be reviewed and should normally have a total of 20 – 40 F1 and F2 training opportunities within it	Establishes procedures for ensuring that local assessments are undertaken in accordance with established assessment procedures	A named and appropriately trained **Educational Supervisor (ES)** will be appointed for each trainee in foundation training
	Ensures that the service needs of the patients and the training/learning needs of foundation trainees are symbiotic and supportive	Ensures that individuals responsible for undertaking assessments have been trained appropriately as part of their professional development	The precise model for this may vary, with the clinical supervisor (see below) and ES being the same individual; or the clinical supervisor and the ES being different individuals and with the ES offering supervision in individual placements, or across either one foundation year or two
		Identifies named Educational Supervisors (ES) for each trainee within the Foundation Programme	Whichever structure is adopted, the ES will have responsibility for: - regular formative appraisal - providing support to the trainee for the development of their *Learning Portfolio* - ensuring that the trainee understands and engages in the assessment process - being the first point of contact for the trainee who has concerns/ issues about their training - ensuring that appropriate training opportunities are made available to learn and gain the required competences
		Ensures that regular appraisal with ES takes place, as a minimum, at the beginning and end of each placement and that trainees' *Learning Portfolios* are properly supported within the appraisal process	An ES should have his/her role formally recognised by having allocated time within their contractual arrangements
		In the two-year Foundation Programmes, ensures smooth progression of trainees from F1 to F2, offering appropriate career management and developmental opportunities	A named **Clinical Supervisor** (who may also be the ES) will be identified for each placement undertaken by the trainee and should have sufficient time available to undertake this role appropriately
		Ensures that individual trainees receive the training required at either F1 or F2 level to meet the competences required	The clinical supervisor will: - supervise the trainee's day-to-day clinical and professional practice - support the assessment process - ensure that the trainee has access to an appropriate range and mix of clinical exposures
		Ensures that the appraisal process is undertaken regularly and appropriately	
		Ensures that the trainee understands the assessment process and engages in it	

	Purpose	Responsibilities	Structure
Foundation School	Under the auspices of the Postgraduate Deanery to: - develop and support the *Operational Framework* within which Foundation Programmes are delivered - provide the *Operational Framework* for doctors who undertake F1 and F2 appointments as well as those who undertake two-year foundation training	Recruitment to foundation training in accordance with Deanery recruitment processes	A **School Director** with credibility in postgraduate medical education should be appointed through a competitive process run jointly by the Deanery and the university/Medical School, with representation from the NHS
		Ensures that fair systems are in place for the allocation of entrants to the School's Foundation Training Programmes	A full-time **Foundation School Administrator** should be appointed to lead the administrative functions, especially in relation to recruitment and appeals
		Communicates with the programmes within the School to ensure that information about Foundation Training Programmes is received regularly and in a timely fashion	Appropriate support staff should be appointed as required to meet the responsibilities of the School
		Coordinates PMETB quality assurance arrangements of Foundation Programme (see below)	A **Foundation School Management Committee** should be established which will be chaired by the School Director and comprise the FTPD/Ts within the School, Deanery, Medical, Medical School, trainee, health services and lay representation
		Develops and manages an appeals system on issues such as recruitment and assessment	

	Purpose	Responsibilities	Structure
Postgraduate Deanery	To set the overall strategy for all Schools/Foundation Programmes in the Deanery in order to deliver foundation training in accordance with national standards set by the GMC and PMETB	Ensures that Schools/ Foundation Programmes have appropriate processes and protocols in place in order to deliver foundation training	**Deanery Foundation School Board** chaired by Postgraduate Dean/s, with membership from the university/ Medical Schools, the NHS, Foundation Schools, patients and trainees
	Is accountable within the NHS for managing the delivery of all programmes to the standards set	Ensures consistency of practice across the Schools/Foundation Programmes in the Deanery	
		Where appropriate establishes a **Deanery Foundation School Board**	

	Purpose	Responsibilities	Structure
individual foundation programmes (ifp's)	A two-year Foundation Programme which is quality assured and competency assessed for eligible graduates	Individual trainees receive the training required at either F1 or F2 level to meet the competences required	Training will be offered within a managed Foundation Training Programme under the auspices of a Foundation Training Programme Director/Tutor
	Training at either the F1 or F2 level, which is not part of a two-year Foundation Programme	The appraisal process is undertaken regularly and appropriately	A named ES will be appointed for each Foundation Programme trainee
		The trainee understands the assessment process and engages in it	
		Through the programme the trainee receives the opportunity for appropriate career management and developmental opportunities	

Section G
Access to foundation training

UK, EEA and other Medical Graduates who are eligible to apply for a two-year foundation training programme

39   **Foundation Training Programmes (FTPs)** offer several kinds of foundation training, providing **individual foundation programmes (ifps)** to trainees:

    i   two-year Foundation Programmes (F1 and F2) open to

- UK medical graduates eligible for provisional registration with the GMC

- medical graduates from the European Economic Area (EEA and Switzerland) eligible for provisional registration with the GMC

- overseas International Medical Graduates (IMGs) who are eligible for provisional or provisional limited registration but are not yet eligible for limited or full registration who therefore require a provisional year of training

    ii   one-year F1 or F2 appointments (or parts thereof)

40   Access to places in Foundation Training Programmes is through a fair and transparent competitive recruitment process across the UK, which is consistent with equal opportunities and employment law. All entrants to Foundation Programmes will need to show that their educational needs are appropriate to the programmes provided by the Deanery/Foundation School.

41   Foundation Programmes and appointments to them should:

- provide training to UK medical graduates who should complete a two-year programme of foundation training, the first year of which, once satisfactorily completed, leads to full registration with the General Medical Council (GMC)

- provide training to EEA and Swiss medical graduates and IMGs who are eligible for provisional or provisional limited registration and are not yet eligible for limited or full registration: such doctors may either undertake a one-year pre-registration appointment (F1) or the full two-year Foundation Programme

- provide training to EEA/Swiss graduates and IMGs eligible for limited or full registration who have appropriate training needs at the level of F2

- allow for any necessary movement between Deaneries and between the four home countries

- help meet the workforce and service needs of the NHS where this is required

42   The two-year Foundation Programme and foundation year one (F1) training will not normally be available to those who are eligible for GMC limited or full registration. However, access to foundation training posts through competition is available to doctors who wish to undertake them and to help fulfil a service need of the NHS.

43   The first year (F1) of foundation training is a pre-registration year required by the GMC for full registration. Doctors in the F1 year will continue to be known as **Pre-registration House Officers (PRHOs)**.

44   The second year of foundation training (F2) is the equivalent to the first year post-registration (currently broadly equivalent to the first year of senior house officer training). The competences to be achieved and assessed during the F2 year are standardised and consistent with the requirements of the Postgraduate Medical and Training Education Board (PMETB) for this level of training. A doctor in the F2 year will be known as a **Senior House Officer 1 (SHO1)**.

Applying for a two-year Foundation Programme

45 Medical graduates as described above who are eligible to apply for a two-year Foundation Training Programme should do so through the following process:

i   A national date will be agreed for the opening of applications to two-year foundation training in the UK. This is likely to be 5th October 2005 for an F1 start in 2006. An advertisement in the medical press will announce that applicants should apply to their first ranked 'Unit of Application' for foundation training.

ii   Deaneries/Foundation Schools will be the 'Units of Application' to which applicants will apply. Applicants will be asked to rank the Units of Application in their order of preference. Entry into the website of the first ranked Unit will offer the applicant the national person specification (Appendix 3) and the local application process. The person specification will enable applicants to identify their personal and educational needs for foundation training and its location so that these can be taken into account. UK medical graduates may elect to apply to a Foundation Programme which is not co-terminus with their university of graduation in order to reflect their own career choices. The opportunity for them to do so should not be discouraged.

iii All applicants will be required to have a letter of support from their own university/Medical School (within or outside the UK), in compliance with GMC requirements (paragraph 52 of transitional edition of *The New Doctor*). This letter will need to confirm that the applicant is considered 'fit to practise' according to GMC standards and will also confirm that this is the only Deanery/Foundation School to which an application is being sent and that the applicant's fitness to practise as a PRHO is not impaired.

iv   Applicants will complete the Unit's application process (either on-line or a paper application), and arrange for the approval letter to be sent.

v   The first ranked School will score the application according to a national scoring scheme. The applicant will carry the score as he/she goes through the recruitment process. The approval letter is not part of the scoring process.

vi   No interviews will be held as part of the admission process to a Unit of Application.

vii Candidates who are not offered a place in their first Unit of Application will automatically have their documentation passed to their second ranked School and so on, until all available places are allocated. If there is an excess of placements over applicants at the end of the process, a clearing round to fill the vacant places will subsequently be held.

viii The outcomes of the application process for August 2006 posts will be announced in mid-January 2006.

ix   It is anticipated that within two - three years, an on-line electronic application process will support this national application process.

46 Some Foundation Schools may choose to allocate a two-year programme at the outset, whilst others may initially allocate F1 training within the School and then subsequently undertake a separate F2 allocation process. Trainees allocated to two-year programmes at the beginning of foundation training should have the opportunity during F1 to consider with their educational supervisor the appropriateness of the second year placements. Where possible, and through a competitive process, the F2 programme element may be changed in the light of this.

47 The application process to two-year foundation training will take into account the exceptional educational and personal needs of graduates where it is possible to do so. Examples of this include primary carer responsibilities, health related issues and specific academic issues.

F1 or F2 appointments: application process for foundation training opportunities which are not part of a two-year Foundation Training Programme

48 The distinction between a two-year Foundation Programme and a F1 or F2 foundation appointment is important. It is anticipated that all UK medical graduates will undertake a Foundation Programme at the end of which they will need to demonstrate both the **required competences (as described in the *Foundation Training Curriculum*) and two years of approved experience**. Trainees undertaking foundation training on a less than full-time basis will need to both achieve the competences and the equivalent of two years whole time experience (see paragraph 90).

49 Entry into a two-year Foundation Programme is also appropriate for doctors with a medical degree granted from a university in the EEA or Switzerland or from overseas and who are eligible for provisional or provisional limited registration but not yet eligible for limited or full registration with the GMC. Such graduates may however wish to apply only for a F1 training opportunity in order to achieve full registration with the GMC. Under these circumstances, these graduates should apply for a full two-year programme through the process described above, but the applicant should make clear at the outset that he/she only requires F1 training. Foundation training opportunities are also available to doctors who already have full registration but who wish to enter training in the UK at a level prior to specialist training. In such cases, entry at the F2 level will usually be the most appropriate point.

50 From time to time F1 and F2 appointments may become available outside the national application process because a vacancy arises. Under such circumstances, in consultation with the employer, the Deanery/School will need to agree how to undertake the recruitment process if one is required. The Foundation Training Programme Director (FTPD) must be involved in the process.

51 It is anticipated that there may be an excess of F2 training opportunities available in some Foundation Training Programmes. The process for competitive recruitment to these will vary from locality to locality, but will be outside the competitive process for two-year programmes.

52 Although doctors in the two-year Foundation Programme should be strongly encouraged to complete their foundation training in the training programme to which they were first appointed, trainees who wish to undertake F2 training in a different Deanery/School will need to apply competitively to do so, unless eligible for an inter-deanery transfer (paragraph 55).

53   All F1 and F2 training opportunities will be educationally managed through Foundation Training Programmes to the same educational standards as the two-year Foundation Programme.

Changing Deaneries/Foundation Schools

54   There are two mechanisms by which foundation training doctors can change to a different Deanery/Foundation School once accepted into one. These are through:

- inter-Deanery transfers for foundation training
- competition (paragraph 84)

Inter-Deanery Transfers for Foundation Training (IDTFT)

55   Foundation training doctors who have special requirements for transferring to a different Deanery once accepted for foundation training should raise these with their Foundation Training Programme Director (FTPD). Transfers will normally take place either at the start of foundation training (F1) or at the start of the F2 year. Arrangements for **Inter-Deanery Transfers for Foundation Training (IDTFT)** must be agreed between Postgraduate Deans on the basis of individual trainee requirements if there are well-founded individual personal or educational needs in relation to, for example:

- health issues
- carer responsibilities
- research opportunities

56   Such transfers will take place only if:

- there are places available in the receiving Deanery
- the applicant has jointly satisfied both Deaneries that there are well-founded reasons for doing so

Medical graduates who start foundation training out of phase

57   Most medical graduates complete Medical School training in July and anticipate starting foundation training in the August after their graduation. However, there is currently a significant and regular cohort of medical graduates who will need to start foundation training at a time other than in August of each year, and who are therefore 'out of phase' in their training.

58   One group includes those graduates who are out of phase because they attend Medical Schools with a **planned** graduation date other than July, which means that they do not start foundation training in August. This is currently the case in one Medical School, which does however intend that its undergraduate programme will be 'in phase' by 2008. Until then the relevant Deanery will enable graduates to compete for foundation training placements that begin at a time compatible with the time of graduation time from Medical School.

59   Another group of graduates may wish Foundation Training Programmes to start at a time other than August for **unplanned** reasons – either because of issues that arose in Medical School, because of unanticipated failure at finals or for personal reasons (e.g. pregnancy).

60 It is anticipated that Postgraduate Deans will work closely with Deans of the Medical Schools (locally and through the Council of the Heads of Medical Schools – CHMS) to ensure that most trainees will eventually start their foundation training in August.

61 Applicants who unexpectedly fail their final examinations will have already applied for foundation training and may have already successfully gained admission to a Foundation School. Under these circumstances they will need to notify the Deanery/Foundation School at the earliest opportunity so that their start date for foundation training can be deferred. These graduates will not normally lose their place in the Deanery/Foundation School but will have their start date deferred to a time agreed with the Deanery. Their original F1 allocation within a programme may not, however, be held and they may be allocated a different training opportunity once they are ready to commence foundation training.

62 Subject to the availability of local resources, Deaneries may offer trainees who have initially failed their finals and then pass them subsequently, three – six months of F1 placements (which may be supernumerary) in order to facilitate their entry into foundation training in the following August. Under these circumstances trainees will then be expected to undertake their full two-year foundation training programme.

Phasing of training

63 It is anticipated that, at some point, agreement to a single start date for F1 training is likely to be reached by the Deans of the Medical Schools and the Postgraduate Deans. However, at the present time graduates who do not begin F1 training in August are out-of-phase with respect to most other UK medical graduates, and, potentially, to the start dates of some specialist training programmes. An approach that Deaneries may adopt in this situation is described in paragraph 62: subject to the availability of local resources, Deaneries may offer trainees who have initially failed and then subsequently pass their finals, three – six months of F1 placements (which may be supernumerary) in order to facilitate their entry into foundation training in the following August. Where this cannot happen because of local resource constraints, some trainees may start their F1 training out-of-phase. Since registration with the GMC takes place after satisfactory completion of the first year of foundation training, these doctors will, in principle, be eligible to move into F2 training, one year after starting F1 training.

64 However, doing so may be neither in their best interests nor in the best interests of the NHS, which is likely to want synchronised starts for F2 training.

65 Those graduates who achieve registration after F1 out-of-phase will therefore normally have three options with respect to foundation training, all of which are subject to local arrangements within the Foundation School and the local NHS:

Option one: upon registration, trainees may commence their F2 training out-of-phase if such an opportunity is available in the Foundation School and the local NHS.

Option two: apply for F2 training opportunities (locum appointments) which might be available at the desired time, either in their home Deanery or elsewhere. If the latter, then trainees would be able to return to their home Foundation Programme to undertake their planned F2 training programme in phase.

Option three: continue in their Foundation Programme and undertake a further six months at F1, acquiring further competences and experience and then enter into F2 in phase.

66   Options two and three gives the out-of-phase starter the opportunity to undertake additional foundation training in order to get 'back into phase' if they wish to do so. Some Deaneries/Foundation Schools may identify other strategies to help support graduates who need to start out-of-phase.

Allocation of F1 and F2 training opportunities following entry into a two-year Foundation Training Programme

67   Acceptance into a two-year Foundation Programme by a Deanery/School does not necessarily guarantee access to a particular F1 training opportunity in that School; although in some Deaneries/Schools selection will be directly into a designated F1 placement. Some Deaneries/Schools may also choose to allocate the placements to the full two-year programme at the outset. Others will allocate initially only to a F1 training opportunity with a later allocation to F2. All of these models are acceptable.

68   Where allocations are not made to a full two-year programme at the outset, the School will ask trainees to express and rank preferences for their F2 allocation at a point six to seven months into the F1 year. Trainees should discuss possible options with their Educational Supervisors, in advance, to help with their choices. Trainees appointed initially to a full two-year programme may also seek to modify their choices in light of experience in F1 with support from their Educational Supervisors and through a local competitive process (paragraph 46).

Deferring the start of foundation training

69   After a trainee has been accepted to foundation training, they may defer the start of their two-year individual foundation programme (ifp) (for reasons other than failing finals, paragraph 61) with the agreement of their Postgraduate Dean or Foundation Training Programme Director(FTPD). Reasons for this may be personal or educational (e.g. to undertake a BSc). Normally a deferral of only one year will be agreed prior to the start of a two-year Foundation Programme. Deferral of the start of an F1 or F2 appointment which is not part of a two-year Foundation Training Programme will normally only be agreed in exceptional circumstances (e.g. on grounds of health).

70   Trainees will be expected to give at least three months notice of their wish to defer in order to allow their foundation placement to be filled by another trainee.

Section G
Access to foundation training

Leaving a two-year Foundation Training Programme temporarily or permanently

71   Once in a two-year Foundation Programme, some doctors may wish to leave it, temporarily or permanently.

Temporary withdrawal from a Foundation Programme

72   Doctors are expected to complete their two-year Foundation Programme as quickly as possible. Some doctors, however, may seek to take time out of the programme for personal or educational reasons.

73   Foundation Training Programmes should have in place an agreed, written protocol (based on the guidance below) for managing requests for time out of a two-year Foundation Programme. Except in unusual and individual circumstances, this will usually relate to time out after F1 and prior to starting F2. The protocol should include a clear timetable and process for taking decisions about requests and an appeals procedure. The process should be managed at programme level, but all programmes within a Deanery/School should use the same procedures and timescale. Where a trainee has a two-year employment contract with a Trust/s, then agreement from the Trust must also be obtained.

Guidelines for taking Time out of Foundation Programmes (TOFP)

74   Doctors who want time out of their Foundation Programme should, in the first instance, discuss this with their educational supervisor. Although they will be expected to complete their Foundation Programme as quickly as possible, they should not be compelled to do so if they have good reasons for wishing to take time out.

75   Time out of a two-year Foundation Programme will usually only be agreed for a one-year period and not for parts thereof. Time out during F1 or F2 placements will only be considered in exceptional (usually unplanned) circumstances.

76   Doctors will request time out of their two-year Foundation Programme, usually after F1, because they for example:

- want to go abroad to work
- want to go abroad to travel
- have domestic reasons
- have health reasons
- have personal reasons

77   Trainees who take time out of programme where statutory employment rights are involved (e.g. maternity leave) will continue to have full entitlement to those rights.

78   If, after discussion, a doctor decides to go ahead with their request to take time out, then the trainee should complete a **TOFP** proforma (Appendix 5). This should be sent to the Programme Director and reviewed in accordance with the Deanery protocol. The Programme Director will need to receive such requests by the end of the sixth month of the F1 year unless there are extenuating circumstances e.g. new health/personal reasons.

79   If one year out of programme is agreed, the trainee will have, in principle, the right to return to their Foundation Training Programme after that year is over. They will however, be required to participate fully in the F2 allocation process according to the timetable set for the year prior to their re-starting their programme.

80   If a trainee's request for time out has been agreed, but their plans/arrangements change, the Deanery/Foundation School will attempt to identify an appropriate training opportunity at short notice but cannot guarantee to do so.

81   Trainees must inform their Foundation Training Programme Director/Tutor (FTPD/T) of their intention to return to the programme six months prior to the start date of their F2 year by completing their F2 preference request. Failure to take this positive action of returning the request document by the required date will mean that the trainee will **not** have an F2 training opportunity within the Deanery/School on their return. Under these circumstances, the returning trainee would need to apply for an F2 appointment in open competition.

Acquisition of foundation competences outside the UK

82   If a trainee requiring a two-year Foundation Programme takes time out of foundation training to undertake clinical work/training abroad it is possible that such training could meet the requirements of F1 or F2 training in the UK. The following conditions will have to be met (subject to GMC and/or PMETB agreement), or foundation training will need to be completed in the UK:

- The trainee will need to arrange a placement abroad which will deliver training in the F1 or F2 competences required

- The proposed training programme, demonstrating how training for the competences will be achieved, must be prospectively agreed by the university (for F1) and the Postgraduate Dean (who will need to recommend the programme to the PMETB for F2 training) prior to the trainee taking up the placement

- The unit abroad which has agreed to deliver the training will need to agree to use the competency-based assessment programme and to assess the trainee in accordance with the documentation required by that programme

- The university (for F1 training) and the PMETB (for F2 training) will need to agree the proposed arrangements prospectively

Permanent withdrawal from a two-year Foundation Training Programme

83   A trainee may choose to withdraw permanently from a Foundation Training Programme, although before so doing they should receive careful counselling and advice from their educational supervisor, School Director or Postgraduate Dean.

84   Trainees should be strongly encouraged to remain in the Deanery/School to which they were appointed for the whole of their two-year programme. However, some trainees may wish to withdraw from a Foundation Training Programme in order to join another Foundation Training Programme for F2. If they do not meet the criteria for an Inter-Deanery Transfer (**IDTFT**) then they will have to apply through competition (paragraph 54) for an advertised F2 post. Prior to applying, trainees should ensure that they discuss this with their educational supervisor and seek appropriate career advice. It will also be essential to confirm that the new F2 post can deliver training in the competences required by the trainee.

85   Such an application is likely to carry some risk since doctors may have had to apply for and accept F2 training in their own locality/programme before knowing whether they have been successful in obtaining the F2 post for which they have competitively applied.

86   **Foundation trainees need to be aware of the GMC strictures relating to accepting posts and then refusing them, without time for adequate arrangements to be made to meet patient and service needs *(Good Medical Practice, paragraph 41)*. A doctor** who has applied for a F2 allocation in their original Foundation Training Programme or School will be expected to take it up and must not withdraw from it unless there is clear agreement from the School Director to do so. The doctor will be expected to conform to contractual obligations regarding notification of resignation as laid down in national terms and conditions of service.

Trainees needing to undertake less than full-time foundation training

87   Doctors requiring less than full-time training must compete for entry into foundation training on an equal basis with other applicants. Once accepted into foundation training, fair and equitable procedures must be in place to allow doctors training less than full-time equal access to foundation training opportunities.

88   Deaneries and Foundation Schools should be clear about how foundation trainees access less than full-time training once admitted to foundation training. The criteria for access to less than full-time training, funding mechanisms and study leave arrangements should be explicit and fair. Doctors must undertake training on at least a half-time basis in order to comply with the requirements of The European Specialist Qualification Order (1995).

89   The current main reasons for undertaking less than full-time training are:

- disability or ill-health
- caring for an ill/disabled partner, relative or other dependent
- providing care for small children

90   Although trainees undertaking less than full-time foundation training might meet the required competences prior to completing two full years of training, an aggregate **total** of two years whole-time equivalence of foundation training should be completed to meet the UK requirements for all foundation trainees of meeting both the foundation competences and undertaking a two-year experiential foundation training (paragraph 48).

91   Trainees undertaking less than full-time training during foundation training should usually be offered slot-sharing arrangements.

92   It should be noted that out of hours contracts for all F1 and F2 trainees are determined by service needs. Where out-of-hours working is determined by service needs, employing authorities will be responsible for meeting this cost element.

Trainees with the Defence Medical Services

93   The Defence Medical Services have a number of Foundation Training Programmes based on its Ministry of Defence Hospital Units (MDHU) within NHS Host Trust Hospitals (in Northallerton, Peterborough, Frimley Park, Portsmouth and Derriford). These posts are fully integrated into foundation training, carry full educational approval and will deliver the required competences of the Foundation Training Programme. However, the number of placements available does not fully meet the demand for all medical cadet graduates in any one year.

94   The selection and posting/appointing process for these MDHU-based placements will take place in advance of the Deanery recruiting process to allow those medical cadets who do not secure a placement within an MDHU to fully participate in recruitment to Deanery programmes. Those cadets selected for an MDHU placement will undertake the full two-year programme at the MDHU facility.

95   The permission of the relevant undergraduate medical Dean must be obtained for application/entry into one of the MDHU schemes, as required by the GMC for all medical graduates.

96   Sign-off for GMC registration for military personnel following satisfactory completion of F1 and confirmation of satisfactory completion and acquisition of F2 competences should be undertaken locally using the same processes and procedures as for their civilian colleagues.

Academic opportunities during foundation training

97   The Academic Careers Sub-Committee of *Modernising Medical Careers* and the UK Clinical Research Collaboration has considered ways in which foundation training can contribute to the academic development of doctors in training, especially during F2. It has stated that 'such academic opportunities during F2 require clearly defined strategic objectives and educational outcomes. The key strategic objective is to develop the academic workforce. A distinction should therefore be drawn between F2 trainees who have already made a career decision to pursue a research/educational career, and those who want the opportunity to explore a potential interest in a research/educational career.' The Sub-Committee therefore recommended that two models of academic training be considered during F2.

i   **Integrated academic F2 programme for trainees wanting to pursue an academic career**

The strategic objective for this route is to provide appropriate training for those trainees who wish to explore the potential for an academic career (including research and education) or wish to make a firm decision to commit to an academic career and make a positive contribution to developing the academic workforce. Selection into this programme should be recognised as a potential precursor to the full development and participation in a defined academic pathway, although it should not be a necessary precondition for entering into that pathway at a later date. Selection to such a programme will be through the competitive route described above for selection into foundation training (although the timing may differ).

The integrated academic F2 programme will consist of an F2 year that has an underlying academic theme so that there is academic activity throughout the year (e.g. an academic mentor, attendance at academic departmental meetings, project work and a taught component). This year may include a focused and protected four months of academic work.

It should be noted that achievement of F2 clinical and generic competences is an essential outcome of this integrated academic F2 programme, since all doctors will need to demonstrate these competences before moving on to specialist training. Academic F2 placements must therefore be designed to allow experience, learning and assessment of these competences.

Academic outcomes should be specifically agreed, along with the support to enable them to happen, at the outset of the placement.

These may include:

- development of skills needed to write grant proposals to pursue a higher degree

- participation in a research/educational project

- sustained academic relationships leading to further joint working (after the placement is completed)

- successful outcomes to a taught component of the programme

Competitive selection of individuals will therefore need to reflect a process that identifies doctors who are not only able to take on the academic challenges but also have acquired well-developed clinical skills relatively early in their foundation training. These appointments should be awarded competitively, to clearly defined, rigorous selection criteria. The competition may be at either local Deanery level or, if a Deanery so wishes, through nationally advertised competition. The local Deaneries and universities/Medical Schools/other eligible academic institutions should make appointments jointly, with each Deanery having an academic lead, in accordance with local processes. The selection process should also involve an NHS representative, to ensure that the programme is organised to balance the academic needs of trainees with the service requirements of the NHS Trusts.

In parallel to this one-year academic F2 programme, there should be the opportunity for **two-year integrated academic Foundation Programme** to be developed by Medical Schools and Deaneries. Such opportunities will be of particular (but not exclusive) value to MBBS-PhD graduates, since it will be possible to accommodate their needs for continued contact with the research base throughout the Foundation Programme. However it may also be desirable for two-year academic programmes to be piloted for other suitable graduates. These programmes will be appointed to on a competitive basis.

ii Stand-alone four-month F2 academic rotations

The aim of such placements is to offer the F2 trainee the opportunity to explore their potential interest in a research or educational career. These may be of particular value to provide exposure to academic subjects that have been less sought after, such as the surgical specialties, pathology, radiology, public health and psychiatry. They may also provide opportunities to participate in programmes for those interested in medical education. As with the integrated academic F2 programme, it will be essential that strategies be identified locally to enable F2 trainees participating in the stand-alone four-month academic rotations to meet the required F2 clinical and generic competences.

Selection to F2 programmes that contain a four-month academic placement will be subject to the same arrangements for allocation of other F2 placements in a Deanery, taking into account the educational needs and aspirations of individual trainees wherever possible, within available resources.

Medical graduates from the European Economic Area (EEA and Switzerland) and from overseas wishing to undertake foundation training

98   In accordance with *Modernising Medical Careers*, all UK medical graduates should undertake a two-year Foundation Programme. Satisfactory completion of the pre-registration year (F1) will lead to full registration with the General Medical Council.

99   Other doctors who are eligible to access such two-year programmes on a competitive basis are those doctors who are eligible for provisional or provisional limited registration with the GMC but are not yet eligible for limited or full registration with the General Medical Council. All doctors eligible for a two-year Foundation Programme (UK medical graduates, EEA and Swiss graduates and doctors from overseas who are eligible for provisional or provisional limited registration with the GMC but are not yet eligible for limited or full registration) will therefore apply through the same competitive process (paragraph 39).

100   Doctors who are already eligible for limited or full registration are not normally eligible for the two-year Foundation Programme. They may apply for competitive entry directly into specialist training is they wish to do so.

101   It is however possible for doctors from outside the UK to apply for either F1 or F2 appointments, through a competitive process to be managed locally through the Foundation Training Programme Director (FTPD) on behalf of the Deanery/School. Doctors who undertake either are eligible to apply competitively for entry into specialist training if they wish to do so.

102   Where an F1 training opportunity is competitively obtained, the Deanery/School may also wish to offer, at the same time, an opportunity for the appointed doctor to participate in a full two-year Foundation Training Programme. The appointed doctor is under no obligation to accept the offer of a full two-year programme of training, but must at the outset indicate whether he/she accepts a one or a two-year programme.

Disabled trainees and trainees with health issues

103   Disabled doctors or with specific health issues (e.g. blood-borne infections) will need to compete for Foundation Training Programmes/appointments. Applications from disabled doctors or from doctors with health issues will be treated in accordance with equal opportunities legislation.

104   Once appointed to a placement, the particular needs of such doctors will require assessment by the Occupational Health Department of the employing Trust to determine whether appropriate arrangements can be put into place to enable the work and training required to be performed.

Trainees requiring additional educational support during foundation training

105   The outcomes and competences required by the GMC and PMETB to complete foundation training are laid out in *The New Doctor* and in the *Curriculum for the Foundation Years in Postgraduate Education and Training*.

106   The GMC and PMETB will agree an assessment process to help doctors in foundation training develop their skills and competences, as well as to formally demonstrate that these have been obtained.

107   Where foundation trainees are not able to demonstrate progress in achieving the outcomes required in *The New Doctor* during F1, they should seek help from their Educational Supervisor and Foundation Training Programme Director (FTPD). Guidance on monitoring PRHOs' progress is set out in *The New Doctor*. They may require referral back to the Medical School from which they graduate and their originating deanery (paragraph 201).

108   The Postgraduate Dean will develop, in conjunction with the relevant Medical School, appropriate remedial processes to support F1 trainees in achieving the required F1 outcomes leading to registration with the GMC. A remedial training placement will be arranged for a fixed period, usually six months. Exceptionally, one further fixed-term extension may be agreed to a maximum of a further six months. If, however, after the period of remediation, a PRHO is unable to demonstrate achievement of the outcomes required by the GMC for full registration, then the GMC 'would not expect PRHOs to continue in practice if they have failed to meet the outcomes within two years' *(The New Doctor, 2005, paragraph 102)*.

109   If a doctor achieves registration with the GMC but during F2 cannot demonstrate progress in developing the competences required, then appropriate action will be required. The trainee will need to seek the support of his/her educational supervisor and Foundation Training Programme Director (FTPD) (see paragraph 205).

110   Provided that the trainee has engaged in the process of training and assessment, and has attempted to address the shortcomings identified, an extension to F2 training may be agreed at the discretion of the Postgraduate Dean.

111   At the end of a period of remediation, if the trainee has not demonstrated the necessary progress, the Postgraduate Dean should undertake a review process which conforms to the arrangements in each of the four home countries. Its function will be to review the local remediation process to ensure that it has been appropriate.

Section I
Approval of educational programmes

Identifying Foundation Training Programmes

112 Foundation Training Programmes will be uniquely identified by a number that will also enable numbering of the F1 or F2 year within that programme. (Each year is composed of a series of three, four or six month placements which will not be uniquely identified.) The format will be similar to that used for national training numbers of SpRs. The number is attached to the posts in the programme and is not allocated to a trainee.

113 One or more Foundation Training Programmes may exist within Trusts. Where one or more Trusts is involved in offering foundation placements in a Foundation Training Programme, the Foundation School/Deanery should identify a Lead Trust for the Programme in order to facilitate educational arrangements for the Foundation Training Programme.

114 Foundation Training Programmes will have between 20 – 40 F1 and F2 year-long training opportunities, with the number potentially varying between Programmes even in a single Trust. For example, a Trust might have two Foundation Training Programmes, one with perhaps 35 (15 F1 and 20 F2s) and one with 32 (14 F1 and 18 F2s) training opportunities.

115 The numbering system consists of a series codes, identifying, in turn, the Deanery, the Trust, the Foundation Training Programme number, whether the training opportunity is F1 or F2 and a unique identifier for the year-long series of placements.

116 As an example:

ED/RC662/01/F1/001

ED   = Deanery identifier (Elsewhere Deanery)

RC662 = RC6 is the Trust code, 62 the site identifier
(New NHS Trust, Green Hospital)

01   = Foundation Training Programme number in the trust (programme one)

F1   = Foundation Year one or two (Year one and hence F1 in this example)

001   = unique identifier for this one-year training opportunity/post

117 Such a numbering system will enable each Deanery to uniquely identify its Foundation Training Programmes (a Deanery with say 300 F1 and F2 year long training opportunities will have a total 10 Foundation Training Programmes).

118 A Deanery will need to obtain educational approval for each of its Foundation Training Programmes (10, in the case above) through the GMC/PMETB quality assurance process, rather than for each individual three, four or six month placement within a programme.

Approval of Foundation Training Programmes

119 The Postgraduate Medical and Education Training Board (PMETB) is the Competent Authority, responsible for setting standards of postgraduate medical education and quality assuring the delivery of those standards after a doctor has achieved registration with the General Medical Council (GMC). The General Medical Council (GMC) is responsible for setting the patterns of experience and quality assuring the first year of foundation training until the grant of full registration. The PMETB and the GMC have responsibility for ensuring that Foundation Training Programmes are regularly quality assured and offer education and training which meets the required standards. The Specialist Training Authority (STA) and Joint Committee on Postgraduate Training for General Practice (JCPTGP) remain the competent authority for F2 until September 2005. The STA has established a process to consider provisional approval of foundation training provided by Deaneries until that date.

120 The Postgraduate Deans are responsible for the educational and operational management of Foundation Training Programmes.

121 The Postgraduate Deans are responsible for ensuring that the placements within the Foundation Programme meet the required standards of training, education, appraisal and assessment as set by the GMC (F1) in *The New Doctor*, and PMETB (F2) in *The Standards for Training, for a Curriculum*, and *for Assessment* as set out by the PMETB and available at the PMETB website (*www.pmetb.org.uk*).

122 Foundation Training Programmes will be identified (through unique number identifiers) as the 'units of approval' through which the PMETB and GMC will approve the delivery of foundation training by Postgraduate Deans.

Foundation Programmes that cross Deanery boundaries

123 Some Deaneries will establish training opportunities that are outside Deanery/School boundaries.

124 Where this occurs, the Trust ('linked Trust') involved should normally not have more than two Foundation Schools with which it has such linked arrangements.

125 Deaneries/Foundation Schools which form such linkages should seek to have at least three – six training opportunities at these linked Trusts so that cohorts of trainees from the Deanery/School can be appointed or allocated to them.

126 The Deanery/School within which the linked training opportunities are located (the 'local' Deanery/School) will have responsibility for ensuring the quality and coordination of the education delivered.

127 The training opportunity will be numbered as one of the training opportunities within a Foundation Training Programme in the local Deanery.

128   Trainees allocated to linked training opportunities will undertake their in-work assessments during the course of their placements. Assuming progress has been satisfactory, the local Foundation Training Programme Director (FTPD) or the educational supervisor on behalf of the FTPD will sign off the trainee (at either the F1 or F2 level) at the end of the year.

129   The Deanery/Foundation School to which the foundation trainee belongs (the 'home' Deanery/School) will be notified of the outcome of the assessment by receiving the **Certificate of Experience** at the end of the F1 year as required by the GMC, or at the end of F2, the **F2 Achievement of Competences Document (FACD).** If the home Deanery is not the same as that from which the trainee graduated Medical School, the Certificate of Experience at the end of F1 will need to be forwarded to the appropriate Medical School (paragraph 196).

130   Trainees in linked training opportunities who experience difficulties in their training will be supported initially by the local Training Programme Director. If concerns cannot be resolved, then the relevant home Deanery/Foundation School will need to be contacted so that a remedial programme can be developed through the home Deanery/School, if required. Although this may take place in the local Deanery, arrangements for this should be made in conjunction with the trainee's home Deanery/School. If additional funding to support remediation is required then the costs for this should normally (but not invariably) be the responsibility of the home Deanery/School.

131   Trainees that choose to, and are successful in competing for an F2 placement outside their original Deanery/Foundation School become the responsibility of the new Deanery/School which they enter. The F2 Achievement of Competence Document (**FACD** – See Appendix 8) will be received by this Deanery and not the original Deanery of entry.

Commissioning F1 and F2 training opportunities

132   Within Foundation Programmes, approval of individual F1 training opportunities and the placements within them will rest with the Postgraduate Dean who commissions and recommends approval of pre-registration training (F1) on behalf of the university.

133   In preparation for approval of foundation training, Postgraduate Deans will recommend to the STA/PMETB those F2 training opportunities that can deliver the range of competences required of foundation training. The STA/PMETB, as the competent authority, will give educational approval to foundation training which has been assessed as delivering the required standard. The Postgraduate Dean commissions this training.

134   Once approval for the F1 and F2 training opportunities within a Foundation Programme has been granted by the GMC/PMETB, the Deanery will be able to make adjustments to the content of individual placements either in order to meet the needs of the overall Foundation Programme or to meet the needs of individual trainees, where this is appropriate and possible. The Deanery will need to notify the GMC/PMETB of this modification between periods of formal approval.

135 Specialty-specific approval of foundation placements is not required since training undertaken during F2 will not be offered prospectively towards specialty training accreditation.

136 It may be that individual trainees choose to request that some of their F2 training be taken into account towards specialty accreditation at a future date, once they have been appointed to a specialty training programme. It will be up to the PMETB to decide the merits of such a request retrospectively.

Shape and content of Foundation Programmes

i   *General Practice*

137 In addition to the defined competences required of foundation training, placements during foundation training should also encourage the foundation trainee to experience of range of specialties.

138 **There is a commitment in principle for all foundation trainees to have the opportunity to undertake a significant experience in general practice during their foundation training.** From August 2006, 55% of trainees in F2 should have general practice placement. The Committee of GP Education Directors (COGPED) is developing this work. A three- or four-month placement during foundation training is the preferred model for arranging experience in general practice. The Royal College of General Practitioners has proposed specific aims and objectives for such a placement. These are described in Appendix 6. Postgraduate Deans and GP Directors, in conjunction with colleagues in general practice will work to identify suitable placements and resources to extend the availability and access to general practice training during foundation training.

This model should also be used, where capacity and resource can be identified, to support placements in shortage priority specialties that have not, in the past, customarily had significant numbers of basic training opportunities. As a result there has been little capacity to date to create F2 placements in these areas. New training opportunities, where possible, should be identified to enable foundation trainees to gain experience in these areas. Where such placements are identified, Postgraduate Deans should approve a programme with clear aims and objectives, describing clearly how the placement will contribute to the development of the foundation competences for a trainee undertaking such a placement.

ii   *Embedded taster experience*

139 Study leave time may be used to develop experiential placements in specialties that trainees wish to explore (paragraph 164). The purpose of such a placement is potentially two-fold:

   i   to give F2 trainees some understanding of what the specialty could offer as a future career, including research and educational academic tasters

   ii   to engender an understanding of the specialty and its contribution to the care and safety of patients

140 These placements may be developed on an ad hoc basis as trainees and their Educational Supervisors identify the aspiration and need to explore specific specialties, or they may be previously established placements in a Trust. Plans to undertake an 'embedded' or 'taster' experience should be made early in the placement so that there is time for them to be appropriately developed on an *ad personam* basis, if necessary. The placements should be planned with local specialists. A detailed timetable that encourages full clinical participation by the trainee should be developed for the placement. Although foundation doctors will clearly need to work under supervision, as F2 trainees they are fully registered and they should therefore be able to make a contribution to the specialty they are exploring, albeit as a supernumerary trainee for the duration of the embedded experience. Well-developed placements will ensure that there is regular senior involvement with the trainee in order to encourage enthusiasm, an interest and an understanding of the specialty. A template for developing an embedded/taster experience placement is shown in Appendix 7.

141 **Placements modelled to allow more than one specialty at a time** to be undertaken during the same time period, e.g. acute medicine combined with medical microbiology. These placements will be subject to the needs of the service and to local arrangements but must contribute to the overall objectives of foundation training and have the Postgraduate Dean's approval.

142   The *Curriculum for the Foundation Years in Postgraduate Training and Education* has been agreed by the competent authorities, but will be kept under regular review. The *Curriculum* will cover both years of foundation training and accordingly, defines the outcomes for F1 as set out in *The New Doctor* as well as the competences required for F2.

143   Postgraduate Deaneries are responsible for ensuring that:

- each foundation trainee has access to an **individual foundation progamme (ifp)** which is a series of placements delivered through the Foundation Training Programme to enable the core competences of foundation training to be achieved

- the placements for each year of the two-year programme will normally (but not invariably) be configured in each year to deliver access to two or three different clinical settings, with three four-month placements per year likely to be the most common (but not the required) model as programmes develop

- the majority of trainees experience training in general practice, subject to resource constraints, with planned expansion in placements over time

- the core professional learning programme described in paragraph 148 – 157 above is delivered, where possible, in an interactive and interprofessional setting

- in approving Foundation Training Programme placements, the totality of the experience, exposure and training will enable the trainee to both acquire and demonstrate through in-work assessment programmes that the foundation competences have been achieved

Educational coherence in foundation training

144 The Postgraduate Deanery will need to ensure that all Trusts/healthcare facilities providing foundation training offer a learning environment that enables and supports F1 and F2 trainees. Both the GMC and the PMETB require this for foundation training approval.

145 The development of the learning environment will need to be enhanced and sustained as foundation training develops. Throughout the UK the Postgraduate Deans have developed educational standards with those organisations with which they commission postgraduate education, through an Educational Contract or Service Level Agreement. An indicative model is shown in Appendix 4.

146 Establishing educational coherence across the two years of foundation training will be important if the programmes are to offer robust and focused outcomes for trainees.

147 For a number of trainees, the location of F1 and F2 training may be geographically disparate. Educational coherence of foundation training can be supported and enhanced through several educational strategies, for example, through:

- named Foundation Training Programme Directors (FTPD) for each Foundation Training Programme who, in addition to Educational Supervisors, will provide support for trainees within the programmes over the whole of a one or two-year programme

- a clear and agreed formal professional generic learning programme delivered to the same national timeframe over the two years of F1 and F2

- use of the National *Learning Portfolio*

- the use of common assessment tools across F1 and F2 and across the UK

Formal teaching programme for the development of professional skills during F1 and F2

148 A key aim of the *Modernising Medical Careers* programme is to ensure that foundation trainees acquire generic skills i.e. those skills that every doctor should have, whatever their specialty or place of work.

149 A formal generic professional programme is therefore part of foundation training and has been specified within the *Curriculum* for both F1 and F2. This programme should emphasise two of the key themes of foundation training – patient safety and accountability through clinical governance.

150 Trainees, trainers, NHS Trusts, educationalists and patients should be assured that the learning programme overtly concentrates on the themes of patient safety and accountability which are at the heart of foundation training.

151 Whilst this learning programme should provide a sufficiently broad framework to encourage variation in the delivery of local programmes, it will support educational coherence across geographical boundaries and will be delivered in all Deaneries to an agreed timeframe. In time, e-learning developments are likely to provide additional educational benefits for foundation trainees.

152 All foundation trainees should register on the **National Patient Safety Agency (NPSA)** interactive educational website *(http://www.npsa.nhs.uk/health/resources/ipse)*. This will enable the reflective educational material offered on the site to be an integral part of foundation training and to form part of the foundation *Learning Portfolio*.

F1 professional learning programme

153 F1 core professional training should be characterised by:

- a uniprofessional interactive programme based on the learning programme below

- equivalent of a minimum of seven days/annum (equivalent to one hour/week) from the currently protected learning opportunities for pre-registration doctors: delivered as full days or as a number of hours/week as part of pre-registration training in accordance with the Dean's educational contract with health service providers

- IT training as necessary through the Trust training department

154 At a minimum the following learning programme should be delivered during F1; the topics emphasising patient safety and accountability through clinical governance:

- understanding clinical governance and its accountability framework

- the evidence and frameworks required to ensure patient safety

- safe prescribing in clinical practice

- clinical accountability and risk management

- legal responsibilities in ensuring safe patient care

- using time effectively to improve patient care

- recognising diversity and gaining cultural competence

F2 professional learning programme

155   F2 training should be characterised by the following:

- interprofessional interactive sessions wherever possible and appropriate

- minimum of 10 days/annum of study leave in the F2 year to support the generic professional learning programme and other aspects of F2 training

- time and funding support from available study leave resources to support the goals of generic professional training programme

- a clinical audit project

- the opportunity to sample additional career alternatives outside F2 placements

156   At a minimum the following learning programme should be delivered during F2:

- decision making through communication with patients

- teamworking and communication with colleagues

- understanding consent and explaining risk

- managing risk and complaints and learning from them

- ethics and law as part of clinical practice

- using evidence in the best interest of patients

- understanding how appraisal works to promote life-long learning and professional development

- taking responsibility for the future of the NHS: teaching others effectively

157   The structured F1 and F2 professional learning programme, spread over the two years of foundation training, is based on developing a generic learning programme with patient safety and accountability as its central theme. The approach also supports improved team-working, another key aspect of foundation training, by promoting interprofessional learning through F2 where this is possible.

Trainees in foundation year one

158 F1 trainees (PRHOs) are not eligible for study leave, although subsequent to registration, the terms and conditions of doctors in training indicate that doctors in training are eligible to apply for study leave in order to augment their postgraduate training, subject to the needs of the service.

However, *The New Doctor* stipulates that 'training must provide regular, formal educational sessions that cover topics of value and interest to PRHOs'.

Postgraduate Deans' educational contracts with Trusts normally recommend up to three hours/week of formal training for pre-registration doctors, at least one hour of which is specifically for meeting the educational needs of the pre-registration doctor.

Trainees in the F1 year must therefore have protected time allocated to support their learning outcomes as laid down by the GMC and the foundation training *Curriculum*, either through a weekly and timetabled learning programme, or possibly by aggregating at least one hour per week of pre-registration training to provide a minimum of seven days per annum for generic professional development in accordance with the generic professional learning programme described above.

Trainees in foundation year two

159 F2 trainees (equivalent to first year SHOs) have access to up to 30 days study leave/annum, consistent with maintaining essential services.

160 COPMeD Study Leave Guidelines recommend that study leave should normally be used to:

- enhance clinical education and training

- be planned as far in advance as possible as an integral part of the education and training process

- provide education and training not easily accrued in the clinical setting or locally

161 Both the GMC and PMETB have defined generic areas of professional competence relating to *Good Medical Practice* and to the *Curriculum*.

162 These areas of competence form some of the key learning objectives of the Foundation Programme. Study leave for F2 should therefore be used to support these learning objectives.

163 A minimum of 10 days/annum (and the proportionate funding per trainee) should be allocated to support a formal educational programme in generic professional training and other aspects of F2 training. The funding allocation for trainees should be used to help support the delivery of the professional programme described above by funding educational activities such as outside speakers, simulation programmes, and administrative support for F2 programmes.

Section L
Study leave during foundation training

164 The remaining time and funding should be used to support other aspects of foundation training, relating to its specific objectives (e.g. ATLS training) and competences. For example, a legitimate use of the time would be to support special interest or embedded taster programmes in diagnostic or other clinical areas in order to explore career alternatives (including academic tasters) not available in a trainee's F2 rotation (see paragraph 136).

Study leave should not be required for the purposes of supporting specialist examinations during foundation training, but could be used to undertake activities to enhance trainees' *Learning Portfolios*.

165 In line with good educational supervision, the foundation trainee should agree with his/her educational supervisor how study leave should most effectively be used to support the aims of the programme, acquisition of the foundation outcomes/competences, the exploration//enhancement of career opportunities and the trainee's wider professional development.

166 By August 2005 the Postgraduate Deans will publish a National *Foundation Learning Portfolio* through the Conference of Postgraduate Medical Deans in the UK (COPMeD). This will be available for the start of foundation training in August 2005. All foundation trainees undertaking foundation training will be required to maintain their *Portfolio* and use it actively to support their educational and professional development.

167 The *Portfolio* is the cornerstone of the foundation training educational appraisal process. Educational appraisal of foundation trainees must take place for every foundation trainee on a planned and regular basis.

168 As in all training and workplace environments, educational appraisal is at the core of good support systems. During foundation training, medical graduates will be making a crucial transition from being a student to entering the workplace of the NHS. They will need regular support to consolidate the skills and knowledge gained in Medical School whilst adapting to a demanding working environment.

169 The Foundation Training Programme Director (FTPD) is responsible for ensuring that each foundation trainee is allocated a trained educational supervisor who may also be the trainee's clinical supervisor.

170 Educational Supervisors must undertake regular and planned appraisals with foundation trainees. They should be trained in how to undertake educational appraisal and give feedback (e.g. *www.appraisal-skills.nhs.uk* offers on-line appraisal training for trainers and trainees).

171 The National *Learning Portfolio* will be designed to facilitate the educational appraisal process, whilst encouraging an approach that fosters adult learning, which is objective-based, self-directed and reflective. Both trainees and Educational Supervisors will need to learn how to use the *Portfolio* to optimise its benefit. During their induction programme, time should be set aside to ensure that trainees understand how the *Portfolio* is used as part of the educational process during foundation training.

172 Deaneries/Foundation Schools will be responsible, in conjunction with the NHS, for ensuring the development of a locally based **foundation training faculty**.

173 Educationalists, skilled in adult learning and in postgraduate medical education, will lead the development of this Faculty although the process will be challenging. It is however fundamental to achieving the aims of the *Modernising Medical Careers* programme.

174 A number of national training days in assessment have been run during 2005 to help support the development of a foundation training faculty and both Deaneries and Colleges continue to offer 'training the trainers' programmes. However, by August 2007, with the implementation of the new edition of *The New Doctor*, all doctors involved in clinical and educational supervision will be required to demonstrate that they have been through a programme that has enabled them to achieve the educational competences required to undertake such supervision.

175 At a minimum, educational and clinical supervisors will have had to demonstrate their competence in educational appraisal and feedback and in assessment methods, including the use of the specific in-work assessment tools approved by PMETB and agreed for use in foundation training.

176 Those who have specific responsibility for giving career advice will also need to be trained in this area.

177 Training in appraisal, competency assessment and career management can be undertaken through a range of training modalities e.g. facilitated programmes provided by Colleges, Deaneries, Trusts or other sources, on-line learning programmes or self-directed learning programmes. Strategies to demonstrate the competences of their Faculty will need to be devised by Deaneries.

Clinical and educational supervision

178 All foundation doctors must have a named educational and clinical supervisor for each foundation placement or part of a placement as appropriate (Table one). The same person often provides clinical supervision and education supervision. Arrangements that separate educational and clinical supervision are acceptable provided they are properly managed and that relevant information about progress and performance is exchanged on a regular basis.

179 Educational Supervisors must be specifically trained for their role and must have explicit time in their contracts and job plans to allow for educational supervision of trainees. Sufficient time must be identified in consultant contracts and job plans to allow senior doctors to undertake clinical supervision whilst meeting their service targets and objectives.

180 Foundation Training Programme Directors (FTPD) have responsibility for ensuring an over-arching structure of supervision spanning the two-year programme where this is within a single geographical locality. Where trainees move to a different locality this responsibility becomes that of the new FTPD.

181 Healthcare organisations should explicitly recognise, in their strategic planning, that supervised training is a core responsibility of the NHS, to ensure both patient safety and the development of the medical workforce to provide for future service needs. The commissioning arrangements and educational contracts developed between Postgraduate Deans and educational providers should be based on these principles and should apply, in the four home countries, to all organisations that are commissioned to provide postgraduate medical education.

Clinical supervision

182 All clinical supervisors should:

- be fully trained in the area of clinical care and understand their responsibilities for patient safety

- offer a level of supervision of clinical activity appropriate to the competence and experience of a foundation trainee and appropriately tailored for the individual trainee

- ensure that no trainee is required to assume responsibility for or perform clinical, operative or other techniques in which they have insufficient experience and expertise

- ensure that foundation trainees only perform tasks without direct supervision when the supervisor is satisfied that they are competent so to do; both trainee and supervisor should at all times be aware of their direct responsibilities for the safety of patients in their care; as fully registered doctors, F2 trainees should be clear about their legal responsibilities with respect to patient care

- consider whether it is appropriate to delegate some supervision to appropriately experienced and trained colleague consultants/general practitioners or non-consultant career grade doctors, in some circumstances: the clinical supervisor remains responsible and accountable for the care of the patient and for the supervision of the foundation doctor in training

- be appropriately trained to teach, provide feedback and undertake competence assessment of foundation trainees

Clinical supervision and the hospital at night

183 Safe and effective clinical care at night requires that hospitals (and integrated healthcare systems) establish multidisciplinary and multi-professional teams. Foundation trainees should be included in these teams where it is appropriate to do so. Safe clinical care will be maintained with appropriate induction (cross-specialty when cross-cover required), managed hand-over and a clear team understanding of individual competences. Strong leadership is a requirement, with overall responsibility residing with a named consultant working in partnership with a night nurse co-ordinator. The foundation trainee should form an important member of such a team but clinical supervision needs to be appropriate.

184 The move to full shift working, especially where there are small numbers of doctors on the rota, could profoundly restrict a doctor's access to clinical supervision. Dedicated senior supervision of emergency work is mandatory in all such circumstances where foundation training doctors might be involved, during all shifts whether out-of-hours or not.

Educational supervision

185 All Educational Supervisors should:

- be adequately prepared for the role and have an understanding of educational theory and practical educational techniques e.g. have undertaken formal facilitated training or an on-line training programme such as *www.clinicalteaching.nhs.uk*

- be trained and accredited as competent to offer educational supervision and undertake competence assessment for foundation training

- offer a level of supervision and review appropriate to the foundation trainee: foundation trainees should expect regular review, and planned reviews through educational appraisal by the educational supervisor

- be responsible:

  i   for ensuring that trainees whom they supervise maintain appropriate records of assessment; and

  ii for contacting the relevant Foundation Training Programme Directors (FTPD) should the level of performance of any foundation trainee give rise for concern

186   Foundation training should offer F1 and F2 trainees the opportunity to explore career options. In addition to rotating through a range of specialties and settings, foundation trainees need access to advice and accurate information about current and future career opportunities. They will also need support, advice and coaching to help plan their careers.

187   Career planning will entail foundation trainees learning and being coached about how best to align their aptitudes, strengths and interests with the needs of the NHS. Robust workforce information, as well as clarity about career pathways, is essential. Good career planning will also involve helping trainees understand that life-long learning is at the core of a successful career, enabling flexibility and adaptability throughout their medical working lives.

188   Deaneries must ensure that those who provide career advice and coaching are trained appropriately. It will not be sufficient for Educational Supervisors to offer informal career advice, as has often occurred in the past. From August 2005 Deaneries will receive funding to support the development of a robust career advisory service which will entail the provision of appropriate advice and information by trained career advisors.

Section P
Assessment during foundation training

189   Assessment of identified competences during foundation training is a cornerstone of the *Modernising Medical Careers* programme.

190   The information obtained through the foundation assessment process is likely to be used to support revalidation of the doctor and must be fit to do so. All trainees will be expected to maintain and develop the *Foundation Learning Portfolio* as evidence of achievement that is used to support the appraisal process and to document progress.

191   The structure of the *Portfolio* reflects the emphasis in foundation training of in-service learning, complemented by a programme of in-service assessment.

192   Using validated assessment tools, trained assessors from a range of healthcare professionals will regularly undertake in-work observational assessments of foundation trainees to a standardised protocol of assessment.

193   The *Curriculum* also indicates that other assessment tools may be used, such as assessment of the *Learning Portfolio*, video assessment or critical incident analysis. These may vary from Deanery to Deanery but in all cases the method of assessment must be made clear to the trainee at the outset of training.

194   The key principles of the assessment process are that it is:

- competence based
- trainee led
- based on in-work assessment
- an open and transparent process
- developmental
- summative

195   The assessment methods will sample from the list of prescribed competences, across their breath and settings. Educational Supervisors and Foundation Training Programme Directors (FTPD) will need to ensure both that trainees can readily arrange assessments during their foundation placements and that assessors are accessible and able to provide assessments at appropriate opportunities.

196 The outcomes of Foundation Programme assessment are:

- **Trainees in F1**
  The areas of competence identified by the GMC in *The New Doctor* will need to be demonstrated in order that full registration of the doctor can be recommended to the GMC. **A Certificate of Satisfactory Service** must be issued at the end of each placement, describing the outcomes achieved. **A Certificate of Experience for PRHOs** will need to be signed off at the end of the PRHO year by the university (or those delegated by the university) from which the F1 trainee graduated.

- **Trainees in F2**
  The trainee will provide evidence, from the in-work and other assessment methods described in the *Curriculum* document, that the F2 competences have been demonstrated through the assessment strategy. The summative assessment process at the end of F2 will need to confirm that the identified competences have been met. The **F2 Achievement of Competence Document** (FACD) will be signed off at the end of F2 for trainees completing the F2 year satisfactorily.

197 Ultimately, the Conference of Postgraduate Medical Deans in the UK (COPMeD) anticipates that a National Assessment Board will be established, enabling the in-work assessments for each trainee to be centrally collated and analysed electronically across all of the clinical and assessment domains, providing a coordinated summative assessment process for foundation training.

Section Q
When a trainee fails to make progress during foundation training

198 Although it is anticipated that most foundation trainees will enjoy their foundation training and be successful in achieving the required competences, some new doctors will struggle. Doctors in this situation may be identified by, for example:

- their reluctance/failure to participate in educational processes
- reluctance/failure to engage fully in the assessment process
- concerns raised by Educational Supervisors
- serious incidents/events/complaints

199 Educational Supervisors should be alert for these and other early signs of problems, and be ready to offer a source of pastoral support to new doctors who are having difficulty adjusting to the role. It is essential that the educational supervisor raises such issues early and formally with the trainee concerned. The educational supervisor should also seek early advice from the Foundation Training Programme Directors (FTPD). The guidance set out in *The New Doctor* must be followed.

200 It may be necessary to arrange an in-depth assessment, looking at health, attitudes, skills and the training environment, in order to take appropriate supportive action.

201 The Postgraduate Dean, or their deputy, and the originating university (for PRHOs) may need to become directly involved so that appropriate remedial or additional assessment measures can be taken (paragraphs 105 – 111). Such action may be in parallel with or as part of the employing authority's performance or disciplinary procedure.

202 *The New Doctor* (transitional edition) sets out guidance on monitoring the progress of PRHOs (*The New Doctor*, 2005, paragraphs 99 – 103).

203 *The New Doctor* indicates that those doctors who cannot achieve the outcomes required for registration during the first foundation year should usually be given remedial support for up to one additional year, but for doctors working full time, 'in normal circumstances, we (GMC) would not expect PRHOs to continue in practice if they have failed to meet the outcomes within two years' (*The New Doctor*, 2005, paragraph 102).

204　While the vast majority of trainees entering Foundation Programme Year two will complete it satisfactorily, some will not.

205　The possible reasons for failure to complete F2, and the options open to the trainee in each situation, may be summarised as follows:

i　**Resignation from an F2 placement or post**

　　This may be for personal reasons e.g. taking a career break, change of career.

　　Exit action: It should be made clear to the trainee that resignation from a post or placement normally implies resignation from the F2 programme. Alternatives to resignation should be explored. Sometimes interpersonal difficulties may resolve with a change of placement and a fresh start with a new trainer. If the trainee is determined on this course, he or she should be given an educational supervisor's report indicating the competences achieved while in the programme, and the level of performance as assessed at the time of resignation. This report should be filed in the foundation *Learning Portfolio* which the trainee should be advised to keep.

　　Return to training: A trainee who has resigned will not have an automatic entitlement to a placement if he/she decides to return. Return to training will be through competitive entry to the F2 programme. Once the trainee has been appointed, the *Portfolio* may provide a useful basis for an initial learning plan. The trainee will normally be expected to complete the full set of competency assessments following return to training, before being issued with a F2 Achievement of Competence Document (FACD), but credit may be given for time previously completed or competences achieved, at the discretion of the Postgraduate Dean.

ii　**Dismissal from an F2 placement, e.g. for misconduct.**

　　Exit action: Dismissal from one placement in the F2 programme implies dismissal from the F2 programme, and requires appropriate disciplinary procedures to be followed by the employing body. The trainee should be given an educational supervisor's report indicating the competences achieved while in the programme, and the level of performance as assessed at the time of dismissal, as well as a brief statement of the facts about the dismissal. This report should be filed in the *Learning Portfolio*, which the trainee should be advised to keep. Serious consideration must be given to referral to the Regional Director of Public Health for an Alert letter, or to the GMC, depending on the nature and gravity of the behaviour, and whether the doctor's fitness to practise is in question.

　　Return to training: Return to training will be through competitive entry to the F2 programme. Application forms to F2 programmes will normally require disclosure of previous dismissal for misconduct and of any disqualification from practice or specified limitations of practice, or current investigations of fitness to practise, in the UK or elsewhere. Once the trainee has been appointed, the *Portfolio* will provide a basis for the initial learning plan. The fact of the previous dismissal, and the behaviours resulting in this, will be taken into account in setting objectives and arranging supervision. The trainee will normally be expected to complete the full set of competency assessments following return to training, before being issued with a F2 Achievement of Competence Document, but credit may be given for time previously completed or competences achieved, at the discretion of the Postgraduate Dean.

iii **Failure to provide evidence of acquiring F2 competences**

This may be, for example, as a result of failure to engage in sufficient assessments, or to submit the outcomes for analysis.

Exit action: It is the trainee's responsibility to ensure that assessments are carried out in a timely fashion. If, at the end of the F2 year, insufficient evidence has been accumulated, an F2 Achievement of Competence Document (FACD) cannot be issued. The educational supervisor should encourage each trainee to engage in the assessment process, and to report any difficulties in doing so in a timely fashion. The educational supervisor should report failure of the trainee to engage to the Foundation Training Programme Directors (FTPD) who should consider additional in-depth assessment, looking at health, attitudes, skills and the training environment, and the appropriate supportive action. Alternative means of assessment may be considered at this stage. If, despite this support, adequate assessments are not completed, the trainee should be given an educational supervisor's report indicating the competences achieved while in the programme, and the level of performance as assessed at the time of coming to the end of the F2 year. This report should be filed in the *Learning Portfolio*, which the trainee should be advised to keep.

Return to training: This will be through competitive entry to the F2 programme. Once the trainee has been appointed, the *Portfolio* may provide a useful basis for an initial learning plan. The trainee will normally be expected to complete the full set of competence assessments following return to training, before being issued with a certificate of satisfactory completion, but credit may be given for time previously completed or competences achieved, at the discretion of the Postgraduate Dean.

iv. **Failure to achieve F2 competences at the end of the F2 year**

This reflects, for example, situations where assessments reveal failure to achieve the required standard for F2 completion within the expected timescale.

Exit action: While every effort should be made by the educational supervisor to recognise the struggling trainee early, and to provide timely support, some trainees will not achieve the required standard within the expected timescale. Failure to progress should trigger an additional in-depth assessment, looking at health, attitudes, skills and the training environment, and the appropriate supportive action should be taken. If at the end of the F2 year the assessments accumulated indicate that the required standard has not been met, the F2 Achievement of Competence Document cannot be issued. The trainee should be given an educational supervisor's report indicating the competences achieved while in the programme, and the level of performance as assessed at the time of coming to the end of the F2 year. This report should be filed in the *Learning Portfolio*, which the trainee should be advised to keep. Depending on the nature and seriousness of the underperformance, consideration should be given to referral to the GMC.

Remedial training: Provided the trainee has engaged with the process of training and assessment, and attempted to address his or her shortcomings, an extension to F2 training may be granted through a remedial training placement, at the discretion of the Postgraduate Dean. A remedial training placement will be arranged for a fixed period, usually six months whole-time equivalent. Under exceptional circumstances, a further fixed-term extension may be agreed, to a maximum of a further six months whole-time equivalent. A remedial training placement will not require entry via open competition, but will be arranged by the Foundation Training Programme Directors (FTPD), in discussion with the trainee, as far as possible to suit the needs of the trainee (paragraph 109). The *Learning Portfolio* will provide evidence of the competences already achieved, and will provide a basis for the development of a learning plan. The trainee will be expected to complete the full set of competency assessments satisfactorily following remedial training, before being issued with a F2 Achievement of Competence Document.

v **Failure to achieve F2 competences at the end of remedial training**

In this situation assessments reveal failure to achieve the required standard for F2 completion despite an extension for remedial training.

Exit action: While every effort should be made by the educational supervisor to support the remedial trainee, it is possible that some trainees will not achieve the required standard even after an extension for remediation. If at the end of the F2 remedial extension, the assessments accumulated indicate that the required standard has not been met, the F2 Achievement of Competence Document cannot be issued. The trainee should be given an educational supervisor's report indicating the competences achieved while in the programme, and the level of performance as assessed at the time of coming to the end of the period of remediation. This report should be filed in the *Learning Portfolio*, which the trainee should be advised to keep. At this stage the trainee will be referred to the GMC.

Return to training: It is conceivable that after a career break, or experience of working in another setting, the trainee who has failed to achieve the F2 competences despite an extension for remedial training may wish to try again. A return to training at this stage will be through competitive entry to F2 training opportunities. Once the trainee has been appointed, the *Portfolio* will provide evidence of the competences already achieved, and those not achieved despite remedial training, and may provide a basis for the development of a learning plan. The trainee will be expected to complete the full set of competency assessments satisfactorily following the return to training, before being issued with the F2 Achievement of Competence Document (FACD).

206 **Foundation Doctors will gain clear benefit from engaging appropriately in the educational and assessment processes of foundation training.** The responsibilities of the foundation doctor with respect to the in-work assessment programme are that they:

- demonstrate professional behaviour in accordance with *Good Medical Practice*

- seek help from appropriate people to address any problems that may arise

- engage with the processes of education and assessment and demonstrate this engagement by attending educational sessions and by participating in the full range and activities required by the assessment to enable their competences to be signed off

- participate in the career management process set up by the Deanery to enable an appropriate alignment of the foundation doctor's aptitudes and aspirations with the opportunities to practise

Section U
After foundation training

207 Once foundation training has been completed, it is the intention that there will be competition for entry into specialist and general practice training. Drawing on available career planning advice and support, doctors will seek to align their aptitudes and aspirations with the opportunities to practise medicine.

208 In accordance with *Modernising Medical Careers: the next steps*, the specific experiences undertaken by a trainee during foundation training will not dictate their entry into specialist training programmes.

209 Further advice on the process by which this will occur for each specialty will be available in due course.

Appendix 1
The duties of a doctor registered with the General Medical Council

'Patients must be able to trust doctors with their lives and well-being. To justify that trust, we as a profession have a duty to maintain a good standard of practice and care and to show respect for human life. In particular as a doctor you must:

- make the care of your patient your first concern

- treat every patient politely and considerately

- respect patients' dignity and privacy

- listen to patients and respect their views

- give patients information in a way they can understand

- respect the rights of patients to be fully involved in decisions about their care

- keep your professional knowledge and skills up to date

- recognise the limits of your professional competence

- be honest and trustworthy

- respect and protect confidential information

- make sure that your personal beliefs do not prejudice your patients' care

- act quickly to protect patients from risk if you have good reason to believe that you or a colleague may not be fit to practise

- avoid abusing your position as a doctor

- work with colleagues in the ways that best serve patients' interests

In all these matters you must never discriminate unfairly against your patients or colleagues. And you must always be prepared to justify your actions to them.'

All foundation trainees should ensure that they have read *Good Medical Practice* and are fully conversant with its content.

Appendix 2
Model job description for Foundation Training Programme Director/Tutor (FTPD/T)

Accountable to: Deanery/Foundation School/Board

Reports to: The Director of Postgraduate Medical Education (DME)/Clinical Tutor (CT) of the Trust holding F1 contracts (or Medical Director if the FTPD is also the DME or CT – see below)

Tenure: Three years (with review after 12 months)

Job purpose:

The Foundation Training Programme Directors (FTPD) is responsible for the overall management and quality assurance of a Foundation Programme that consists of 20 – 40 placements designed for foundation training across a health economy (Acute, Mental Health and Primary Care Trusts). S/he will work with the local lead educators to ensure that each placement of the programme meets the Deanery standard for training and that each trainee is able to access a comprehensive range of experiences which will enable them to gain the competences necessary for full registration and completion of foundation training. In some Deaneries/Schools it may be appropriate for the Clinical Tutor to also be one of or the Foundation Training Programme Directors (FTPD) since many of the current PRHO and early SHO years roles will be subsumed within Foundation Training Programmes.

Key responsibilities:

1   **To deliver a high quality Foundation Training Programme**

   a   Work with the Foundation Board to ensure that the training programme meets the requirements with Deanery educational contracts for foundation training and the ten principles described in *'Modernising Medical Careers – The Next Steps'*

   b   Work with local lead educators (Clinical Tutor, Course Organiser, and College Tutors) to ensure that each placement in the programme provides high quality experience and meets the educational aims for the programme and those specified for the placement.

   c   Ensure that all educational and clinical supervisors have received appropriate training (including equality and diversity training) for their role as educators and assessors.

   d   Ensure that all Educational Supervisors are familiar with the Deanery and national documentation to be completed prior to registration, completion of foundation training and for revalidation.

   e   Provide annual reports to the Foundation School so that they can be confident that the programme is meeting the expected standard.

   f   When required, produce materials about the programme to ensure effective recruitment to the Schools and to F2 placements.

2 **To organise and ensure delivery of a high quality interactive generic professional programme for all Foundation Trainees and to enable the attendance of foundation trainees in the programme.**

a In conjunction with other Foundation Training Programme Directors (FTPD), determine a local model for delivery of generic professional training to a minimal equivalent of three hours/week (required in deans' educational contracts) for PRHOs (which may be delivered weekly or as full day equivalents, e.g. about seven days of training/annum).

b In conjunction with other Foundation Training Programme Directors (FTPD), determine a local model for delivery of generic professional training to a minimal equivalent of 10 days/annum for F2 trainees.

c In conjunction with other Foundation Training Programme Directors (FTPD), determine what aspects of the specific and generic competences are best taught in a peer group setting and arrange a suitable programme.

d To consider the possibility of creating such programmes in whole or in part to be delivered in an interprofessional context.

e To ensure that the F1 and F2 local generic learning programmes conform at a minimum to the learning programmes laid out in this document and are delivered appropriately in year one and in year two.

f Work with local lead educators and Trust HR Departments to ensure that Trusts are familiar with the timetable for foundation training and that foundation trainees have clinical duties arranged to enable them to regularly attend their generic training.

g To define the educational aims of each session, consider the most effective educational method and most effective facilitator thereby producing a trainee centred interactive educational programme.

h To evaluate each session and the overall programme giving feedback and producing reports as appropriate.

3 **To work with the local Trusts to ensure effective development of Educational Supervisors for Foundation Trainees.**

a To maintain databases of Educational Supervisors including their potential to contribute to the generic professional programme and their preparation for their role.

b To devise an effective method of selection and reselection of educational and clinical supervisors in conjunction with Director of Medical Education/Clinical Tutor, local HR Departments and the Deanery.

4 **To contribute to the overall development of the Deanery**

a To attend development programmes for clinical educators and maintain skills in medical education.

b To lead development projects by mutual agreement and share the results.

5 **To work with other tutors within the Health Economy to ensure foundation training benefits from a co-ordinated approach.**

Appendix 3
Application to enter a two-year Foundation Training Programme

Person Specification

	ESSENTIAL	DESIRABLE	WHEN EVALUATED
Qualifications	Has or is expected to achieve MBBS or equivalent medical qualification		AF
	Has not yet reached the level of experience required for GMC limited or full registration		
Eligibility	Has written approval from university of medical graduation for this application		Approval letter from university
	Has confirmation this is the only first ranking application submitted		Approval letter from university
Fitness to practise	Is up to date and fit to practise safely		Approval letter and Fitness to Practise statement from university
Knowledge & achievements		Academic and extracurricular achievements	AF
		Demonstration of participation in aspects of 'Good Medical Practice'	AF
Education & personal aspects		Educational reasons for applying for this School/Deanery	AF
		Personal reasons for applying for this School/Deanery	AF
Communication & interpersonal skills	Able to communicate effectively in written English		AF
	Able to communicate effectively in spoken English		To be confirmed in testimonial from university
		Evidence of team-working skills	AF
		Evidence of leadership skills	AF
Health	Meets professional health requirements		Pre-employment health screening
Probity	Displays honesty, integrity, respects confidentiality		AF

AF = *Application form, including Personal Statement*

Any attributes which are evaluated on the basis of the application form may be further explored by reference to the applicant's Medical School and at pre-employment screening.

Statement by your Dean/Postgraduate Dean or other appropriate Medical School Official

I give permission for

Name of applicant (please print)

to apply to

Name of Deanery/Foundation School

Deanery or Foundation School and confirm that this is the only Deanery or Foundation School application on the UK National Scheme being submitted by this candidate, which this Medical School has supported. I confirm that the student is of good standing at this Medical School and is considered Fit to Practise medicine in accordance with UK General Medical Council's (GMC) Fitness to Practise requirements as described in the GMC's Good Medical Practice.

I consider the applicant's level of English language to be:

Spoken: Excellent   Good   Acceptable   Poor

Written: Excellent   Good   Acceptable   Poor

Please complete one of these three statements, as appropriate:

I confirm that subject to the outcome of final year examinations, it is anticipated that the medical training undertaken to date by this candidate will entitle the candidate to **provisional** registration according to UK registration requirements.

I confirm that the medical training undertaken to date entitles this candidate to **limited or full** registration in the UK, according to UK registration requirements (required for non-UK medical graduates only).

I confirm that, subject to the outcome of final assessments in this Medical School, it is anticipated that the medical training undertaken will entitle the candidate to **limited or full** registration in the UK, according to UK registration requirements (required for students in certain Medical Schools in the EEA who will graduate with the eligibility to apply for full registration in the UK).

Signed

Stamp/Seal of School

Name

Position

Address

Tel   **Fax**

E-mail

Appendix 4
Postgraduate Dean's model educational standards for doctors in foundation training

Section one:
Overall management/support of foundation training standards

1.1 Foundation training should be reflected in the overall approach to Postgraduate Medical Dental Education (PGMDE) in the Trust. A clear policy document agreed by the Trust Board, setting out the strategic direction of PGME and foundation training as an integral part of it should be available.

1.2 There should be a Trust Educational Committee structure that includes PGMDE and within it, ensures that foundation training is integrated into its policies. The following should be included:

   i Clear Terms of Reference for the overall Committee with arrangements for foundation training clarified. Regular minutes should be kept and circulated to all interested parties.

   ii The Chief Executive, Medical Director and Director of Human Resources are represented on the Committee by a senior member of staff.

   iii All aspects of PGMDE, including foundation training and the pastoral care of trainees are considered.

   iv Foundation Training Programmes Directors/Tutors (FTPD/T) should be appointed to lead Foundation Training Programmes. Normally one FTPD should manage 20 – 40 F1 and F2 training opportunities and the trainees in them. The Clinical Tutor/Director of Medical Education may be a FTPD since many of their current responsibilities with respect to PRHO/F1 and first year SHOs/F2 will be subsumed in the role of FTPD.

   v The Committee is responsible for the development of a doctors' in-training handbook, detailing information on hospital-wide clinical protocols. A specific handbook for foundation trainees may be considered appropriate but at a minimum, guidance for foundation trainees should be included in the doctors' in-training handbook.

   vi Appropriate 'training the trainer' opportunities should be made available locally, or through CPD opportunities, at a minimum in:

   • educational and clinical supervision
   • appraisal
   • competence assessment

   Any healthcare professional undertaking competence assessment of foundation trainees must be trained to do so, either through written guidance, facilitated training or e-line training opportunities.

1.3 Liaison and support from the human resources department should ensure that:

i   Documentation of all training opportunities offering foundation training at either F1 or F2 should be detailed (including part-time posts) and should be kept up-to-date with the Deanery/Foundation Schools database.

ii   The Trust is able to provide information on foundation training doctors as required by the Postgraduate Dean, including equality and diversity data. Where the Trust operates medical manpower computer software, the data should be kept fully up to date.

iii   This information should be available to the Director of Medical Education/Clinical Tutor/Foundation Training Programme Director (FTPD) as required.

iv   There are regular and formal links between the Director of Medical Education/Clinical Tutor/Foundation Training Programme Directors (FTPD)/Deanery and local medical staffing covering all matters relating to the education and pastoral care of doctors in foundation training.

1.4 Annual report on foundation training

i   The Foundation Training Programme Directors (FTPD), in conjunction with the Director of Medical Education/Clinical Tutor must produce an annual report on the progress of foundation training within the Trust/s. This may form part of the annual report that Directors of Medical Education/Clinical Tutors deliver to the Deanery as part of the overall educational contract.

ii   The report should specifically highlight any difficulties with reference to:
   - ensuring that foundation trainees have access to foundation training placements which enable them to develop the foundation competences that are required by the Foundation Training *Curriculum*
   - a taught generic professional programme is developed in line with the *Curriculum* and that foundation trainees are enabled to attend. Where possible, this should be delivered in an interprofessional setting
   - trainers responsible for foundation training having access to training the trainer opportunities in educational supervision, appraisal (including the use of the *Foundation Learning Portfolio*) and competency assessment
   - foundation trainees having access to career support/management programmes
   - difficulties in providing part-time foundation training when required

iii   The report should describe any difficulties with the placement of flexible trainees.

Appendix 4
Postgraduate Dean's model educational standards for doctors in foundation training

Section two:
Employment of doctors in foundation training

2.1 All foundation training doctors should have up to date job descriptions, at each stage of their rotation that should include an outline of the educational programme for their current placement, developed with the help of the Foundation Training Programme Directors (FTPD).

2.2 Opportunities for training must be made available for those unable to work full-time for well-founded personal reasons. In line with recent changes to flexible training arrangements, this will normally be either:

   i   through reduced sessions in established full-time posts or;

   ii by two trainees sharing a substantive training slot, with additional sessional in-put from the deanery ('slot-shares').

   Exceptionally, supernumerary part-time training will be considered where circumstances are such that this is the only way foundation training can be undertaken.

2.3 Foundation training doctors should normally have employment contracts issued prior to taking up their placements, but at a maximum, within four weeks of starting their foundation placement.

2.4 All foundation training doctors should undergo a *hospital* induction programme and a *departmental* induction for each new placement in accordance with EL (94) 1. This must include at a minimum:

   i   An educational induction, offering training in the use of the *Foundation Learning Portfolio* and in the tools used for foundation competency assessment;

   ii In accordance with Department of Health guidance, information on the expected standard of infection control to be practised.

   iii There must be an up to date Hospital Handbook for use by all foundation training doctors which is issued to them on induction, which should contain relevant and up-to-date information on key functions and contact points.

   iv Relevant clinical protocols should be discussed as part of the departmental induction.

2.5 Trusts must ensure that training grade doctors are not bullied or intimidated or subjected to other inappropriate behaviour, which represents an abuse of professional authority.

   i The Deanery/Foundation School must have a Policy on Bullying and Harassment which in turn must require that all Trusts have a Policy on Bullying and that foundation trainees are made aware of it.

   ii Where bullying of foundation trainees is discovered, Trusts must take suitable action independently or with the Deanery and/or the appropriate Royal College. The Deanery is to be informed of the situation and the measures taken.

2.6 All foundation training doctors' hours and work intensity must be in accordance with the requirements of the 'New Deal' and the European Working Time Directive. Foundation trainees should participate wherever appropriate in the Hospital at Night and other team-working initiatives, under appropriate supervision.

Section three:
Foundation trainees – inappropriate duties

3.1 Inappropriate duties must not routinely be carried out by foundation trainees e.g. delivering requests/samples for investigations, phlebotomy, chasing X-rays. Appropriate secretarial and ward clerk support must be provided to support foundation trainees in their service and educational work.

3.2 Duties such as clerking for endoscopy lists (day cases), day case surgery or angiography (day cases) must only be carried out by trainees when such work forms an educational and/or natural part of the continuity of patient care.

3.3 Tasks such as exercise ECGs and minor surgery are only appropriate for foundation trainees to carry out if there is a clear training component, i.e. supervision by a more senior doctor or further involvement in the patient's care.

Section 4:
Educational activities

4.1 All foundation training placements must have the Postgraduate Dean's approval. This includes those academic appointments that are recognised for foundation training.

Appendix 4
Postgraduate Dean's model educational standards for doctors in foundation training

4.2 **The educational infrastructure for foundation training should be supported by the following:**

i   All foundation trainees should be made explicitly aware of three core educational documents which directly affect their training:

       1   *Good Medical Practice (GMC)*

       2   *The New Doctor (GMC)*

       3   *Curriculum for the foundation years in postgraduate education and training*

    Copies of these documents should be provided to trainees either by reference to appropriate websites or by hard copy.

ii   Educational Supervisors should agree trainees' educational objectives and these should be written in individual personal development plans (PDPs) within the *Foundation Learning Portfolio*. The PDPs are to be reviewed regularly at the end and beginning of each new placement through a regular appraisal process to ensure steady progress against the require foundation competences.

iii   Within the first week of starting a placement, a meeting between the educational supervisor and the foundation trainee should take place to set educational objectives and to review progress in previous posts/placements.

iv   Advice on career management and planning should be made available to all foundation trainees by senior people trained to do so.

v   There must be evidence of a robust programme of formal education in generic professional and clinical skills designed to address the foundation training *Curriculum*. These may include lecture/tutorial programmes, interactive sessions, departmental meetings, participation in clinical audit, interprofessional learning sessions, training in a simulated environment, e-line learning etc.

vi   Foundation trainees should work under supervision as members of and within clinical teams.

vii   Foundation trainees should also work to the limit of clinical responsibility consistent with a reasonable assessment of their competence and the level of their supervision. This should include active participation in the Hospital at Night and in appropriate out of hours service.

viii   The Trust must ensure foundation trainees are enabled to take agreed study leave that supports the educational objectives of foundation training.

ix   The Trust needs to demonstrate its responsibility for ensuring that the educational responsibilities of foundation Educational Supervisors and trainers are acknowledged within a consultant's employment contract.

x   The Trust needs to demonstrate that foundation educational and clinical supervisors and trainers are enabled to undertake appropriate professional development ('training the trainers') to support their training activities.

4.3 Foundation year one trainees - PRHOs

i   Training for these doctors should reflect the principles recommended in the GMC's *The New Doctor* (1997) (but recognise that developments should support the implementation in 2007 of the *The New Doctor* (2005).

ii There must be relevant supervised and protected structured training in accordance with the university/Deanery guidelines so that a Certificate of Experience can be issued at the end of F1.

iii There must be an educational programme aimed at F1 training needs of at least one hour a week, which they can attend in protected (bleep-free) time. There should be another two hours a week (also in protected, bleep-free time) of relevant formal education. There must be evidence of a robust programme of formal education in generic professional and clinical skills designed to address the foundation training *Curriculum*. This time can be aggregated to offer full days of training where this meets local conditions.

iv There must be a comprehensive and appropriate induction process for PRHOs whenever they start a placement in a new site or department.

v   There should be arrangements in place for appropriate career support and management for F1 trainees.

vi Formalised assessments of F1 performance should take account of progress towards:

  • satisfying the outcomes of F1 training, as set out in the GMC's *The New Doctor*

  • conforming to the requirements set out in the GMC's guidance on *Good Medical Practice* for all doctors.

4.4 Foundation year two trainees (SHO1)

i   Training should reflect the principles and competences reflected in the foundation training *Curriculum* and agreed by the PMETB.

ii Relevant and protected formal education programmes for trainees in F2 must be in place during working hours. The Dean requires that at least three hours/week of protected, relevant formal education is provided.

iii Trainees in F2 training should be enabled to learn the skills and attitudes recommended in the *Curriculum* through service-based learning.

iv F2 trainees should agree their objectives and personal development plans with their Educational Supervisors during their appraisal meetings. F2 trainees should receive regular constructive feedback and appraisal on their professional performance and progress in achieving the foundation competences during each of the F2 placements.

v   Appropriate career counselling support and management must be available for F2 trainees through senior people trained to do so.

Appendix 4
Postgraduate Dean's model educational standards for doctors in foundation training

Section five:
Study leave during foundation training

5.1 **Professional or study leave should be granted for the purposes of supporting the objectives and outcomes of foundation training.**

   i Study leave should not be required for the purposes of supporting specialist examinations during foundation training.

   ii All trainees are entitled to three hours of 'in-house' formal education as part of their working week, which should be relevant, protected ('bleep-free') and appropriate to either F1 or F2 training. This may be aggregated to release whole days for generic training, during F1 (a total of seven days using one hour/week) or the F1 generic training professional programme can be delivered on a weekly basis. There is no study leave funding centrally available for F1 training.

   iii During the F2 year attendance at foundation generic training programmes is compulsory. Formal education programmes which support generic professional training are part of the trainee's study leave allowance and should offer a minimum of 10 days training/annum, and should cover the areas in the F2 generic professional training as described in the *Curriculum*. Both study leave funding and time available to F2 trainees can be used for this purpose. Study Leave can also be used to support learning about different clinical specialties through embedded taster experiences to support the career exploration component of MMC, as well as an understanding as to how the specialty contributes to patient care.

5.2 **Trainees training flexibly during foundation training are entitled to full financial access to study leave allocations. Time for study leave should be calculated pro rata based on their flexible training commitments.**

5.3 **Individual training objectives, and the study leave associated with these, should take account of the requirements of the *Curriculum* for foundation training and the trainee's personal needs.**

5.4 **As indicated in 5.1 (iii), study leave during foundation training can legitimately be used to support attachments and experience in other specialties.**

Trainee's name:

E-mail address:

Contact address:

Contact telephone number:

Location of current F1 placement:

Identification number of F1 training opportunity:

Name of Educational Supervisor:

Name of Foundation Training Programme Director (FTPD):

Have you discussed your plans to take time out of programme with your Educational Supervisor?

Yes   No

Have you discussed your plans to take time out of programme with your FTPD?

Yes   No

Please give your reasons for wanting to take time out of your Foundation Programme:

Please describe what you hope to do during this time out:

If you are undertaking clinical work/training, do you hope to achieve your F2 competences in this post?

Yes   No

If yes, have you been able to plan a programme to do so?

Yes   No

Please attach a description of the clinical training you will receive in order to achieve the F2 competences.

Is the unit you are planning to go to aware of the assessment programme required to demonstrate the competences?

Yes   No

Are they prepared to undertake such assessments?

Yes   No

Appendix 5
Time out of Foundation Programme (TOFP) request form

Have you applied to the PMETB for prospective approval of the placement?　　　　Yes　　No

If you are not planning on undertaking clinical work that you might wish to have considered by the PMETB for prospective approval, when do you plan on returning to take up an F2 placement in your Foundation School?

Date you wish to start your out-of-programme experience:

I am requesting approval from the Foundation School/Deanery to undertake time out of my Foundation Programme as described above. Please tick the appropriate options below to signify your understanding of the process.

　　I have already applied to the PMETB for prospective approval to ask if my planned clinical programme can be used to demonstrate the F2 competences and to gain the experience required of foundation training.

　　I have already received prospective approval from the PMETB and attach it here.

　　I wish to return to F2 training after my time out of programme. I understand that I must ensure that I apply through the usual process as set out by the Foundation School and meet the required timescales in order to secure an F2 allocation. I understand that if I do not, I may not be allocated an F2 placement in the Foundation School.

Signed		*Foundation Trainee*
Print name		**Date**

Signed		*Educational Supervisor*
Print name		**Date**

Signed		*Foundation Training Programme Director*
Print name		**Date**

After all three signatures have been obtained, one copy should be sent to the Foundation School Director, one copy should be kept by the FTPD and the foundation trainee should retain one copy.

1.0 This document contains extracts from a paper developed by a Working Group (January 2004) of the Joint Committee on Postgraduate Training for General Practice (JCPTGP), which represents all the key stakeholders in general practice education, and the Royal College of General Practitioners (RCGP) to ensure that the discipline of general practice contributes fully to the development of Foundation Training Programmes.

2.0 **Learning outcomes for the general practice period of the Foundation Programme**

2.1 A good way to synthesize these areas of skills acquisition and competence is for learners to follow patient pathways through the service, both in hospital and the community, from the presentation of acute illness, through investigation and diagnosis, management to recovery or rehabilitation. Throughout the attachment, the foundation doctor should consider and reflect on the impact on each patient of the hospital environment, the general practice environment and their interface. Whilst in general practice they should consider the impact of disease on the patient's life within his or her own environment.

2.2 It is important to understand the essential difference between providing a training experience in general practice for all doctors and specialist training programmes for a career in general practice.

2.3 Virtually all of the clinical experience of doctors entering their Foundation Programmes will have been acquired in a secondary care setting. A placement in general practice will provide a valuable contribution to each of the areas described for the second foundation year, and will provide a meaningful experience of general practice in the context of the overall Foundation Programme. It will not be aimed at producing the skills and competences required of the modern general practitioner. For the majority this will be their only postgraduate experience of general practice.

2.4 Thus the general practice foundation placement will offer doctors in training and opportunity to provide care for patients in a very different setting, that of primary care, and in the context of the patients themselves. The patterns of team working are different in primary care, and general practice has a broad and unique perspective on the way in which secondary care specialties work. The manner of presentation of acutely ill patients is different in general practice, and illnesses are seen at a much earlier stage in their development. Their management in this setting requires differing skills both in clinical method and risk assessment.

3.0 **Patients**

During the placement the doctor will:

- gain an understanding of the person-centred approach, oriented to the individual

- work with patients in their own context and community

- gain an understanding of the impact of the patient as a person in a family

- gain an understanding of the physical, psychological, social and cultural dimensions of the problems presented

- gain understanding of the difference between disease and illness

Appendix 6
General practice and foundation training

4.0 Illnesses

During the placement the doctor will:

- see illnesses at an early and undifferentiated stage
- understand the different epidemiology and the prevalence and incidence of illness in the community
- manage simultaneously episodes of new acute illness with concurrent chronic problems in the patients they see
- manage the interface with secondary care through referral, acute admission and discharge from hospital

5.0 Processes

During the placement the doctor will:

- gain an understanding of the advantages of medical generalism in the community setting
- work in, and understand the roles of, the primary care team in providing care to individual patients
- gain an understanding of the importance of effective communication between patient and doctor, and the relationship built over time
- gain an understanding of effective communication between health care professionals and the carers of patients.
- gain an understanding of the role of primary care in promoting health in the community
- learn about decision making and risk management in the absence of support services (pathology, imaging, senior colleagues)
- understand the impact of working at the point of first contact to the health service with open access to patients
- gain an understanding of the impact and analysis of evidence based medicine and its application in the primary care setting
- understand the importance of continually developing personal knowledge

It will not be possible in a short placement to cover all of these issues in any great depth but it should be possible to provide the recently qualified doctor with a meaningful experience, which will greatly contribute to the value of their Foundation Programme.

6.0   Key messages

- Every doctor should experience general practice during his or her Foundation Programme as one of a range of settings in which care for the acutely ill patient is delivered.

- General practice is an important setting for doctors to learn many of the core competences of the Foundation Programme.

- The competences required for the successful completion of this programme should encompass those from general practice as described in this paper.

- The expertise in GP education in synthesizing and supervising educational experiences from different disciplines should be fully utilized by those involved in developing and managing the Foundation Programme.

Introduction to Specialty 'X' – *Curriculum* for F2s

(Indicative duration: one - two weeks. Note: this is only a draft template. Others may be suitable in different clinical or academic settings)

Introduction

These training opportunities should be available (as options) to all trainees in their F2 year. They are particularly suited to those considering specialising in e.g. the diagnostic specialties, certain medical specialties or paediatrics, but will also be of great interest to those considering general practice and most other specialties, including academic work in either research or teaching.

The attachment should be well-planned and focused, with agreed aims to be achieved and an understanding about how the attachment would be assessed. A one-week attachment provides at least 40 hours of specific interaction around *the specialty* issues and a two-week attachment, up to 80 hours. If such attachments are focused they should be able to contribute significantly to the understanding and development of a F2 trainee.

During the attachment, trainees should obtain an appreciation of:

- The way that the specialty **contributes to individual patient management** in a range of settings and for different patient groups, including prevention, diagnosis, treatment and follow-up, and contributes to **health protection**.

- The importance of **infection control and the specialty** in supporting patient safety.

- Optimum **use of diagnostic tests** for common clinical conditions.

- The general principles underlying therapeutics and prescribing in the specialty.

- The scope of **career opportunities** in the specialty, including academic (research and teaching) and managerial potential.

Depending on local circumstance, one or two F2 trainees can be accommodated concurrently in the specialty. However, as such attachments are intended to provide hands-on experience of the specialty, they are not suited to a course or tutorial-based approach.

Educational programme

The F2 trainee should review his/her understanding of the specialty before commencing the placement:

- **Clinical aspects:** the trainee should attend clinical rounds and outpatients with senior trainees or consultants, including the ITU, SCBU and specialist units where appropriate to learn how the specialty works in practice and to understand how the specialty contributes to the care and safety of patients. The F2 trainee is a fully registered doctor and should make a contribution to the care of patients under supervision even on a short attachment.

- **Diagnostic aspects:** the F2 trainee should become conversant with diagnostic aspects of the specialty in order to learn how to use resources more effectively and appropriately.

- **Management aspects:** the trainer should select a small number of real-time clinical cases that demonstrate common but important problems in the specialty and use the cases to explore the diagnosis, management, review and follow up of the patient over the duration of the attachment. The training experience would include presentation of cases at the departmental clinical meeting.

- **Health protection and prevention aspects:** the trainer should select examples from clinical cases that promote health protection and prevention and ensure that these aspects are discussed.

- **Academic opportunities in the specialty, where available, in research and in teaching should be included.**

Contribution of attachment to the development of F2 competences

There is likely to be considerable scope for such an attachment to support the trainee in the development a number of areas of F2 competence:

- help develop a range of **clinical competences** supported by understanding the better use of diagnostic and managerial approaches in the specialty; how to approach the 'undifferentiated' patient, opportunity to see and interact with a range of clinical conditions and other specialties

- contribute to the development of an understanding of **clinical priorities** and their management

- support the development of **communication and team-working** by experiencing and participating in the dynamics of the specialty and the other healthcare professionals who work in it

- improved understanding of the **use of resources** and using an **evidence base** for making decisions about these

- support an understanding of **health promotion** as well as healthcare and support generic principles around such issues as **patient safety** (from the viewpoint of the specialty) and **infection control** in the specialty

- improved skills in **case development** and **presentation skills**

- potential for **academic development** opportunities if individual trainees wish to develop/continue an academic relationship with the department

Assessment

The attachment trainer and trainee will need to agree with the Educational Supervisor the specific aims (e.g. as above) of the attachment. Achievement of these and the contribution of the experience undertaken/knowledge gained will be evaluated through an end of attachment discussion so that the contribution to the development of specific competences is the specific focus of the trainers' report. The trainer is in an ideal position to observe at first hand the skills and performance of the trainee around the specific areas indicated above. The trainee should also inform this by a written piece of reflective work identifying the agreed aims and saying how he/she believed these had been achieved in order to help the development of insight and understanding into their own performance.

Appendix 8
Foundation Achievement of Competency Document (FACD)

Foundation Achievement of Competency Document (FACD)

Name of trainee:	**GMC No:**
Trust:	**Start Date:**
Placement 1 Specialty:	**Educational/Clinical Supervisor:**
Placement 2 Specialty:	**Educational/Clinical Supervisor:**
Placement 3 Specialty:	**Educational/Clinical Supervisor:**

Documentation to be considered :
a) Portfolio   b) Attendance at formal teaching sessions
c) Record of study leave   d) Record of sickness

Has the trainee developed an up-to-date Portfolio?   ☐ Yes   ☐ No

Has the trainee completed the required assessments
in each of the three posts?   ☐ Yes   ☐ No

Has the trainee met the requirements laid down in the GMC,
the New Doctor and the Foundation Programme curriculum?   ☐ Yes   ☐ No

Additional comments from Educational Supervisor:

Additional comments from trainee:

I confirm that Dr
has satisfactorily demonstrated the competences required of foundation training.

Signed

Educational Supervisor/RITA Chair/External Assessor

Print name   **Date**

Final decision by Foundation Programme Director

Signed:

Trainee

Delete as applicable:

Has **achieved** the requirements of the Foundation Programme

Has **failed to achieve** the requirements of the Foundation Programme

Signed:

Foundation Programme Director

Print name: **Date:**

Signed:

Trainee

Print name: **Date:**

This document should be sent to your Deanery/Foundation School and a copy should be placed in your Learning Portfolio.

Appendix 9
Glossary of terms

Appraisal	A positive process to provide feedback on the foundation trainee's performance, chart their continuing progress and identify their developmental needs (after *The New Doctor, transitional edition*).
CHMS	Council of the Heads of Medical Schools and Deans of UK Faculties of Medicine.
Clinical Supervisor	The professional responsible for teaching and supervising the foundation trainee (after *The New Doctor, transitional edition*).
COGPED	Committee of GP Education Directors.
Competence	The possession of requisite or adequate ability; having acquired the knowledge and skills necessary to perform those tasks which reflect the scope of professional practices. It may be different from **performance**, which denotes what someone is actually doing in a real life situation. (*from the Workplace Based Assessment Subcommittee of the PMETB*)
Competences	The skills that doctors need (after *The New Doctor, transitional edition*).
COPMeD	Conference of Postgraduate Medical Deans in the UK.
Curriculum	A *curriculum* is a statement of the aims and intended learning outcomes of an educational programme. It states the rationale, content, organization, processes and methods of teaching, learning, assessment, supervision, and feedback. If appropriate, it will also stipulate the entry criteria and duration of the programme (from the *Workplace Based Assessment Subcommittee of the PMETB*).
Educational Supervisor	The doctor responsible for making sure that the foundation trainee receives appropriate training and experience and who decides whether individual placements have been completed successfully (after *The New Doctor, transitional edition*).
F1	The first foundation year which follows on from Medical School graduation and which is prior to registration with the General Medical Council (GMC).
F2	The second foundation year; follows registration with the GMC.
FACD	F2 Achievement of Competence Document. Awarded to the foundation doctor at the end of foundation training to indicate that the foundation competences have been successfully achieved.

Foundation Training Programme (FTP)	The 'unit of approval' which will be quality assured by the Postgraduate Medical Education and Training Board. A FTP will normally consist of between 20 – 40 F1 and F2 foundation training opportunities and will be led by a Foundation Training Programme Director/Tutor (FTPD/T). All foundation training will take place within Foundation Training Programmes.
Foundation Training Programme Director/ Tutor (FTPD/T)	The individual appointed by the Deanery and Trust/s to manage and lead a Foundation Training Programme.
GMC	General Medical Council. Responsible for the General and Specialist medical register in the UK in which a doctor must be included to practise medicine in the UK. Has strong and effective legal powers designed to maintain the standards the public have a right to expect of doctors.
Individual foundation programme (ifp)	The specific Foundation Training Programme followed by an individual trainee, consisting of a series of clinical placements that enables the trainee to gain experience and training in the competences required.
Interprofessional	People from different professions (for example, doctors and nurses) working or learning together (after *The New Doctor, transitional edition*).
JCPTGP	Joint Committee on Postgraduate Training for General Practice. The current competent authority for general practice training (until September 2005)
PMETB	Postgraduate Medical and Education Training Board. Will take on the responsibilities as the competent authority for both hospital specialties and general practice from September 2005. An independent body with responsibility in law for setting standards and quality assuring postgraduate medical education in the UK.
Posts	These are the training opportunities contracted with trainees by healthcare organisations during their individual foundation programmes at either F1 or F2 level.
Placements	The clinical components of an individual foundation programme, typically consisting of three specialties in either a F1 or F2 post.
PRHO	Pre-registration House Officer; a first year (F1) foundation trainee.

Professionalism	Adherence to a set of values comprising statutory professional obligations, formally agreed codes of conduct, and the informal expectations of patients and colleagues. Key values include acting in the patients' best interest and maintaining the standards of competence and knowledge expected of members of highly trained professions. These standards will include ethical elements such as integrity, probity, accountability, duty and honour. In addition to medical knowledge and skills, medical professionals should present psychosocial and humanistic qualities such as caring, empathy, humility and compassion, social responsibility and sensitivity to people's culture and beliefs. (*from the Workplace Based Assessment Subcommittee of the PMETB*).
Programme	A managed educational experience.
SHO1	Trainees in the second year of foundation training; this is first year post-registration with the GMC.
STA	Specialist Training Authority. The current competent authority for hospital specialist training (until September 2005).
TOFP	Time out of Foundation Programme.

Operational Framework for Foundation Training

The *Operational Framework* is a working document and we welcome your feedback. Should you have any feedback for the next revision, please write to our Operational Framework Co-ordinator at **operationalframework@mmc.nhs.uk**

Or write to:
Operational Framework Co-ordinator
Modernising Medical Careers
6th Floor
New Kings Beam House
22 Upper Ground
London
SEW 9BW

Curriculum for the Foundation Years in Postgraduate Education and Training

The *Curriculum for the Foundation Years in Postgraduate Education and Training* is also a working document. Should you have any feedback for the next revision, please write to the Chair of the AoMRC Foundation Committee at **foundationcommittee@aomrc.org.uk**

Or write to:
Chair of the Foundation Committee
Academy of Medical Royal Colleges
1 Wimpole Street
London
W1G 0AW

✳ HISTORY ✳ VIEWPOINTS ✳

ALFRED

THE GREAT

AND THE ANGLO-SAXONS

DAVID GILL

W
FRANKLIN WATTS
LONDON • SYDNEY

Franklin Watts

Published in Great Britain in paperback in 2018
by The Watts Publishing Group

Copyright © The Watts Publishing Group 2016

All rights reserved.

Series editor: Julia Bird
Series designer: Matt Lilly
Picture researcher: Diana Morris

ISBN 978 1 4451 6205 8

Printed in China

FSC
www.fsc.org
MIX
Paper from
responsible sources
FSC® C104740

Franklin Watts
An imprint of
Hachette Children's Group
Part of The Watts Publishing Group
Carmelite House
50 Victoria Embankment
London EC4Y 0DZ

An Hachette UK Company

www.hachette.co.uk
www.franklinwatts.co.uk